Pre-Algebra

Best Value Books™

Table Of Contents

The student pages in this book have been specially prepared for reproduction on any standard copying machine.

Kelley Wingate products are available at fine educational supply stores throughout the U. S. and Canada.

Pre-Algebra **CD-3731** Printed in the United States Of America ISBN 0-88724-449-1

About the book...

This book is just one in our Best Value™ series of reproducible, skill oriented activity books. Each book is developmentally appropriate and contains over 100 pages packed with educationally sound classroom-tested activities. Each book also contains skill cards and resource pages filled with extended activity ideas.

The activities in this book have been developed to help students master the basic skills necessary to succeed in mathematics. The activities have been sequenced to help ensure successful completion of the assigned tasks, thus building positive self-esteem as well as the self-confidence students need to meet academic and social challenges.

The activities may be used by themselves, as supplemental activities, or as enrichment material for the mathematics program.

These math practice pages were developed by teachers and tested by students. We never lost sight of the fact that if students don't stay motivated and involved, they will never truly grasp the skills being taught on a cognitive level.

About the author...

Dawn Talluto Jacobi holds a Bachelor's degree in Mathematics. While raising her three children (Eric, Kaitlin, and Matthew) Dawn found herself in demand as a math tutor. She noted a common thread that kept children from finding success in math classes—a lack of self-confidence. Dawn developed a game format that attracted and held her students' attention because it made math more fun. Dawn discovered that she enjoyed teaching and decided to enter the field full time. She is currently teaching high school Algebra and is working on her Master's degree in Education.

Senior Editors: Patricia Pedigo and Roger DeSanti
Production Director: Homer Desrochers
Production: Arlene Evitts and Debra Ollier

 CD-3731

Ready-To-Use Ideas and Activities

The activities in this book will help students master the basic skills necessary to become competent learners. Remember as you read through the activities listed below and as you go through this book, that all children learn at their own rate. Although repetition is important, it is critical that we never lose sight of the fact that it is equally important to build students' self-esteem and self-confidence if we want them to become successful learners.

The back of this book has removable flash cards that will be great for basic skill and enrichment activities. Pull the flash cards out and cut them apart (if you have access to a paper cutter, use that). Use the flash cards to practice and reinforce algebraic concepts. Always remember to tell students the number of problems that were answered correctly. For example, if the student answers 7 problems correctly out of ten, tell the student that he or she got 7 problems correct, not "you missed three." Building self-confidence and fostering good feelings about learning are very important.

Adding Real Numbers

Positive + Positive = Positive
$5 + 3 = 8$
Negative + Negative = Negative
$-7 + (-4) = -11$
Positive + Negative or Negative + Positive
Keep the sign of the larger number and subtract.

Multiplying and Dividing Real Numbers

Positive x Positive = Positive
$3 \times 4 = 12$
Negative x Negative = Positive
$(-2) \times (-1) = 2$
Positive x Negative or Negative x Positive = Negative
Positive ÷ Positive = Positive
$24 \div 4 = 6$
Negative ÷ Negative = Positive
$(-15) \div (-3) = 5$
Positive ÷ Negative or Negative ÷ Positive = Negative

Ready-To-Use Ideas and Activities

Make a priority pyramid like the one below to remind students to perform operations in the correct order.

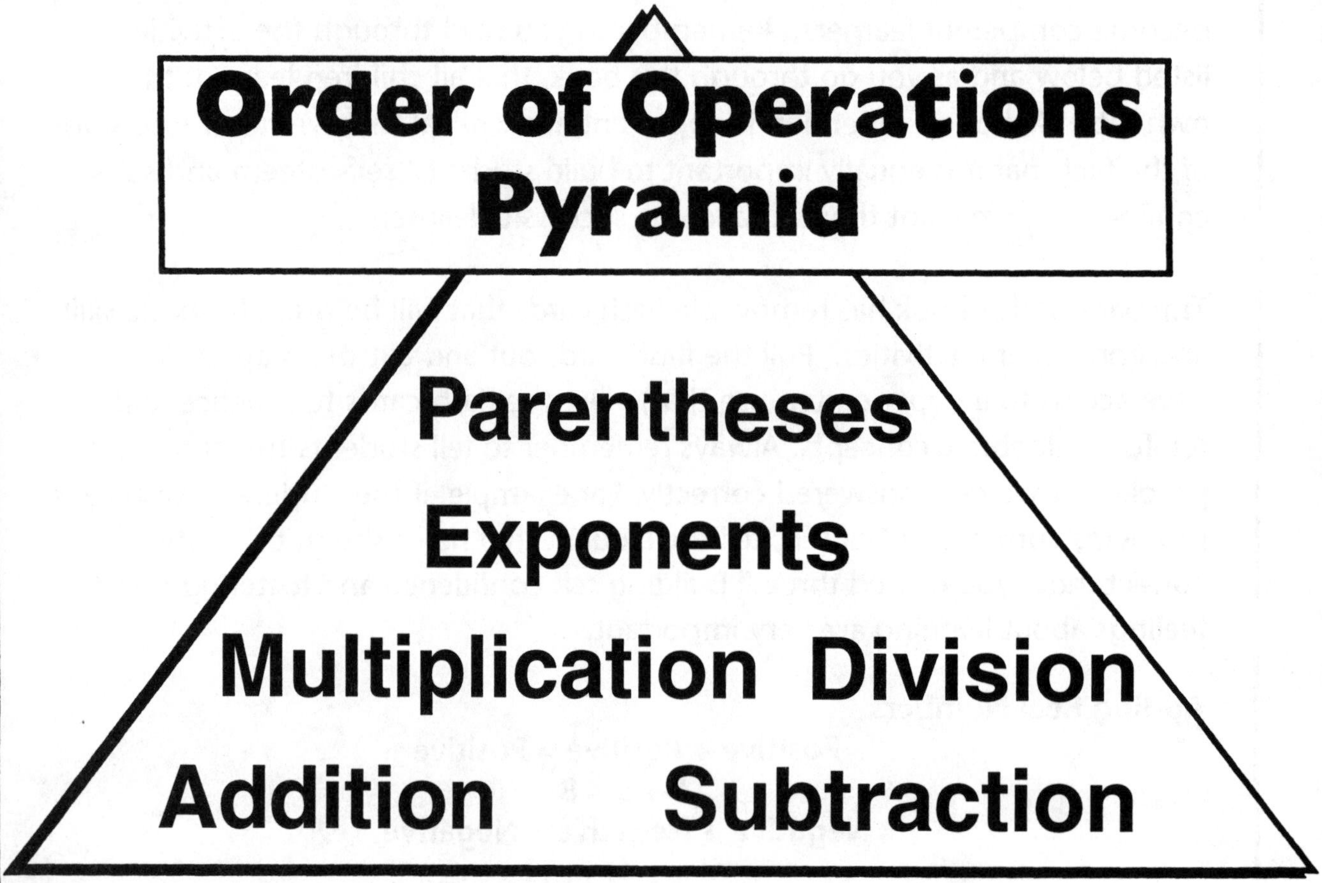

Memory Mate

The following is a fun way to remember the Order of Operations.

Please Excuse My Dear Aunt Sally

P for Parentheses
E for Exponents
M for Multiplication
D for Division
A for Addition
S for Subtraction

If a problem presents operations with the same priority, such as multiplication and division, simply perform all operations from <u>left to right</u>.

Ready-To-Use Ideas and Activities

Rounding

To round to a certain "place" simply locate the place to which you are rounding and:

1. Draw a line under that digit.
2. Draw a circle around the number to the right of the underlined digit.
3. This circled number will tell you what to do:

   If the circled number is a 0, 1, 2, 3, or 4, it is telling the underlined digit to **stay the same.**

   If the circled number is a 5, 6, 7, 8, or 9, it is telling the underlined digit to **increase by one.**

4. After the circled number "tells' the underlined digit what to do it becomes zero and disappears if it is after a decimal point.

Example:

Round to the nearest tenth.

128.453

128.$\underline{4}$53 (the circled number "tells" the underlined number to increase by one.) the answer is 128.5. Notice that the circled number now becomes zero and disappears.

Changing Fractions to Decimals

To change a fraction to a decimal simply divide.

Remember that $\frac{\mathbf{3}}{\mathbf{4}}$ means "3 divided by 4"

$$\begin{array}{r} 0.75 \\ 4\overline{)3.00} \\ \underline{-28} \\ 20 \\ \underline{-20} \\ 0 \end{array}$$

Changing Decimals to Fractions

Always remember that the number of places behind the decimal is the same number of zeros in the denominator.

0.7 is seven tenths or $\frac{\mathbf{7}}{\mathbf{10}}$

Simplifying Fractions

$$\frac{3}{6} \div \frac{3}{3} \text{ (greatest common factor)} = \frac{1}{2}$$

1. $\frac{6}{9}$

2. $\frac{19}{57}$

3. $\frac{10}{70}$

4. $\frac{13}{39}$

5. $\frac{8}{24}$

6. $\frac{6}{21}$

7. $\frac{6}{39}$

8. $\frac{6}{15}$

9. $\frac{57}{63}$

10. $\frac{32}{136}$

11. $\frac{9}{36}$

12. $\frac{45}{72}$

13. $\frac{35}{55}$

14. $\frac{4}{36}$

15. $\frac{30}{45}$

16. $\frac{21}{36}$

17. $\frac{56}{74}$

18. $\frac{12}{18}$

19. $\frac{56}{63}$

20. $\frac{7}{49}$

21. $\frac{16}{72}$

Simplifying Fractions

$$\frac{14 \div 2}{12 \div 2} = \frac{7}{6}$$

Improper Fraction

$$\frac{14 \div 2}{12 \div 2} = \frac{7}{6} = \frac{6}{6} + \frac{1}{6} = 1 + \frac{1}{6} = 1\frac{1}{6}$$

Mixed Numeral

Write each answer as an improper fraction, then write each as a mixed numeral.

1. $\frac{63}{18}$
2. $\frac{45}{27}$
3. $\frac{28}{20}$
4. $\frac{15}{9}$
5. $\frac{36}{24}$
6. $\frac{27}{21}$
7. $\frac{30}{12}$
8. $\frac{69}{18}$
9. $\frac{50}{30}$
10. $\frac{20}{12}$
11. $\frac{28}{24}$
12. $\frac{26}{10}$
13. $\frac{20}{8}$
14. $\frac{45}{36}$

Name________________________________

Adding and Subtracting Fractions

When the denominators are the same, add or subtract the numerators.

$\frac{1}{6} + \frac{2}{6} = \frac{3}{6} = \frac{1}{2}$ $\frac{4}{6} - \frac{1}{6} = \frac{3}{6} = \frac{1}{2}$

Add or subtract as indicated. Reduce to lowest terms.

1. $\frac{2}{7} + \frac{3}{7}$
2. $\frac{17}{18} - \frac{8}{18}$
3. $\frac{13}{24} + \frac{17}{24}$
4. $\frac{11}{15} - \frac{6}{15}$
5. $\frac{3}{21} + \frac{11}{21}$
6. $\frac{16}{17} - \frac{9}{17}$
7. $\frac{11}{12} + \frac{9}{12}$
8. $\frac{19}{20} - \frac{17}{20}$
9. $\frac{4}{15} - \frac{1}{15}$
10. $\frac{7}{9} + \frac{8}{9}$
11. $\frac{31}{32} + \frac{29}{32}$
12. $\frac{15}{16} - \frac{11}{16}$
13. $\frac{13}{15} + \frac{11}{15}$
14. $\frac{32}{35} - \frac{17}{35}$
15. $\frac{16}{18} + \frac{17}{18}$
16. $\frac{19}{20} - \frac{9}{20}$
17. $\frac{19}{24} + \frac{23}{24}$
18. $\frac{23}{25} - \frac{8}{25}$

Adding and Subtracting Fractions

When the denominators are different, find the least common multiple. In this case, 24.

$$\frac{3}{8} + \frac{2}{6} = \frac{9}{24} + \frac{8}{24} = \frac{17}{24} \qquad \frac{3}{8} - \frac{2}{6} = \frac{9}{24} - \frac{8}{24} = \frac{1}{24}$$

Add or subtract as indicated. Reduce to lowest terms.

1. $\frac{1}{6} + \frac{3}{4}$
2. $\frac{3}{4} + \frac{2}{9}$
3. $\frac{7}{8} - \frac{2}{3}$
4. $\frac{6}{7} + \frac{1}{4}$
5. $\frac{7}{10} - \frac{3}{8}$
6. $\frac{1}{3} + \frac{4}{8}$
7. $\frac{1}{2} - \frac{4}{9}$
8. $\frac{1}{6} + \frac{7}{9}$
9. $\frac{5}{8} + \frac{11}{12}$
10. $\frac{9}{10} - \frac{7}{15}$
11. $\frac{2}{3} - \frac{2}{5}$
12. $\frac{2}{4} + \frac{3}{5}$
13. $\frac{5}{6} + \frac{7}{8}$
14. $\frac{9}{25} - \frac{3}{10}$
15. $\frac{3}{8} - \frac{1}{5}$
16. $\frac{5}{12} + \frac{6}{8}$
17. $\frac{4}{9} + \frac{7}{8}$
18. $\frac{8}{9} - \frac{5}{12}$

Name______________________________

Adding and Subtracting Fractions

When the denominators are different, find the least common multiple. In this case, 12.

$\frac{3}{4} + \frac{4}{6} = \frac{9}{12} + \frac{8}{12} = \frac{17}{12}$ $\quad$ $\frac{3}{4} - \frac{4}{6} = \frac{9}{12} - \frac{8}{12} = \frac{1}{12}$

Add or subtract as indicated. Reduce to lowest terms.

1. $\frac{10}{12} - \frac{3}{5}$
2. $\frac{14}{15} + \frac{1}{6}$
3. $\frac{8}{9} + \frac{4}{5}$
4. $\frac{17}{21} - \frac{4}{6}$
5. $\frac{13}{15} - \frac{5}{18}$
6. $\frac{7}{15} + \frac{3}{6}$
7. $\frac{11}{12} - \frac{5}{18}$
8. $\frac{3}{10} + \frac{7}{15}$
9. $\frac{5}{6} - \frac{3}{8}$
10. $\frac{5}{8} + \frac{2}{7}$
11. $\frac{6}{7} - \frac{3}{5}$
12. $\frac{7}{8} + \frac{9}{10}$
13. $\frac{7}{12} + \frac{7}{8}$
14. $\frac{2}{6} + \frac{3}{9}$
15. $\frac{4}{15} - \frac{3}{12}$
16. $\frac{29}{32} + \frac{7}{8}$
17. $\frac{11}{14} - \frac{1}{6}$
18. $\frac{4}{5} + \frac{11}{15}$

Name_______________________________

Adding and Subtracting Mixed Numbers

When the denominators are different, find the least common multiple. In this case, 8.

$$3\frac{1}{4} + 1\frac{3}{8} = 3\frac{2}{8} + 1\frac{3}{8} = 4\frac{5}{8}$$

1. $4\frac{5}{8} - 2\frac{2}{6}$
2. $8\frac{1}{6} + 5\frac{3}{4}$
3. $3\frac{7}{12} + 7\frac{5}{6}$
4. $12 - 3\frac{1}{5}$
5. $1\frac{9}{10} - 1\frac{3}{4}$
6. $5\frac{1}{2} - 2\frac{2}{7}$
7. $9\frac{3}{5} + 4\frac{2}{3}$
8. $16\frac{1}{3} - 7\frac{5}{8}$
9. $4\frac{1}{8} - 3\frac{1}{2}$
10. $12\frac{7}{9} + 3\frac{2}{3}$
11. $4\frac{8}{9} + 2\frac{5}{6}$
12. $3\frac{8}{12} - 1\frac{5}{18}$
13. $7\frac{1}{2} - 2\frac{7}{10}$
14. $6\frac{2}{7} - 1\frac{1}{3}$
15. $17\frac{3}{4} - 8\frac{2}{5}$
16. $6\frac{4}{5} + 2\frac{3}{8}$
17. $11\frac{4}{5} - 3\frac{5}{6}$
18. $4\frac{3}{6} + 7\frac{3}{8}$

Practice Adding and Subtracting Fractions

When the denominators are different, find the least common multiple. In this case, 9.

$$2\frac{2}{3} + 6\frac{4}{9} = 2\frac{6}{9} + 6\frac{4}{9} = 8\frac{10}{9} = 9\frac{1}{9}$$

1. $5\frac{1}{2} - 3\frac{5}{6}$

2. $9 - 6\frac{1}{3}$

3. $7\frac{3}{8} + 4\frac{1}{4}$

4. $12\frac{2}{7} - 3\frac{5}{6}$

5. $8\frac{1}{3} + 6\frac{7}{9}$

6. $15\frac{7}{8} - 4\frac{2}{9}$

7. $7\frac{8}{12} - 5\frac{1}{3}$

8. $14\frac{3}{4} - 8\frac{5}{6}$

9. $3\frac{7}{12} + 6\frac{12}{18}$

10. $5\frac{3}{10} - 3\frac{9}{12}$

11. $10\frac{10}{12} - 3\frac{4}{6}$

12. $9\frac{15}{18} + 5\frac{4}{12}$

13. $5\frac{5}{9} + 3\frac{4}{6}$

14. $8\frac{2}{9} + 3\frac{3}{6}$

15. $6\frac{2}{7} - 5\frac{3}{14}$

16. $9\frac{8}{11} + 4\frac{1}{2}$

17. $13\frac{4}{21} - 8\frac{2}{3}$

18. $7\frac{7}{12} - 3\frac{4}{7}$

Multiplying Fractions

$$1\frac{2}{3} \cdot 2\frac{1}{2} = \frac{5}{3} \cdot \frac{5}{2} = \frac{25}{6} \text{ or } 4\frac{1}{6}$$

(rewrite $1\frac{2}{3}$ as $\frac{5}{3}$; rewrite $2\frac{1}{2}$ as $\frac{5}{2}$)

1. $\frac{3}{5} \cdot \frac{15}{18}$
2. $\frac{2}{3} \cdot \frac{21}{24}$
3. $5\frac{1}{2} \cdot \frac{2}{11}$
4. $7\frac{2}{7} \cdot 2\frac{1}{3}$
5. $5\frac{3}{5} \cdot 2\frac{1}{7}$
6. $3\frac{12}{13} \cdot 4\frac{1}{3}$
7. $4\frac{4}{7} \cdot 1\frac{3}{4}$
8. $8\frac{1}{3} \cdot 6\frac{3}{5}$
9. $3\frac{1}{5} \cdot 12\frac{1}{2}$
10. $1\frac{1}{2} \cdot 3\frac{1}{5}$
11. $9\frac{1}{3} \cdot 2\frac{1}{7}$
12. $2\frac{3}{4} \cdot 1\frac{1}{3}$
13. $4\frac{5}{6} \cdot 5\frac{1}{7}$
14. $12\frac{2}{3} \cdot 7\frac{1}{2}$
15. $5\frac{2}{3} \cdot 8\frac{1}{4}$
16. $10\frac{2}{3} \cdot 7\frac{1}{8}$
17. $2\frac{4}{7} \cdot 2\frac{3}{9}$
18. $5\frac{3}{12} \cdot 2\frac{1}{7}$

Multiplying Fractions

$$2\frac{1}{3} \cdot 1\frac{1}{2} = \frac{7}{3} \cdot \frac{3}{2} = \frac{21}{6} \text{ or } 3\frac{3}{6} \text{ or } 3\frac{1}{2}$$

(rewrite $2\frac{1}{3}$ as $\frac{7}{3}$; rewrite $1\frac{1}{2}$ as $\frac{3}{2}$)

1. $12\frac{1}{2} \cdot 8\frac{2}{5}$
2. $8\frac{3}{4} \cdot 1\frac{3}{7}$
3. $13\frac{1}{3} \cdot 2\frac{2}{5}$
4. $5\frac{5}{7} \cdot 9\frac{4}{5}$
5. $7\frac{1}{8} \cdot 9\frac{1}{3}$
6. $4\frac{2}{3} \cdot 7\frac{1}{2}$
7. $3\frac{1}{3} \cdot 9\frac{3}{4}$
8. $7\frac{1}{3} \cdot 4\frac{1}{2}$
9. $6\frac{2}{9} \cdot 3\frac{6}{8}$
10. $3\frac{3}{5} \cdot 2\frac{7}{9}$
11. $3\frac{8}{9} \cdot 5\frac{2}{5}$
12. $4\frac{7}{12} \cdot 6\frac{2}{5}$
13. $8\frac{2}{5} \cdot 3\frac{4}{7}$
14. $15\frac{3}{4} \cdot 6\frac{2}{7}$
15. $8\frac{4}{5} \cdot 2\frac{5}{10}$
16. $10\frac{1}{2} \cdot 7\frac{1}{3}$
17. $5\frac{4}{9} \cdot 2\frac{4}{7}$
18. $11\frac{2}{3} \cdot 4\frac{4}{5}$

Dividing Fractions

$$1\tfrac{2}{3} \div 2\tfrac{1}{2} = \tfrac{5}{3} \div \tfrac{5}{2} = \tfrac{\cancel{5}^{1}}{3} \cdot \tfrac{2}{\cancel{5}_{1}} = \tfrac{2}{3}$$

(rewrite; rewrite; invert and multiply)

1. $6\frac{2}{3} \div 3\frac{4}{12}$
2. $4\frac{1}{2} \div 5\frac{1}{4}$
3. $2\frac{2}{9} \div 4\frac{1}{6}$
4. $6\frac{2}{3} \div 4\frac{4}{9}$
5. $8\frac{3}{4} \div 2\frac{1}{2}$
6. $7\frac{3}{5} \div 1\frac{9}{10}$
7. $3\frac{1}{3} \div 1\frac{5}{9}$
8. $4\frac{3}{8} \div 2\frac{1}{12}$
9. $9\frac{2}{7} \div 2\frac{2}{14}$
10. $7\frac{1}{5} \div 3\frac{3}{5}$
11. $7\frac{3}{4} \div 1\frac{1}{4}$
12. $5\frac{2}{5} \div 4\frac{1}{2}$
13. $2\frac{7}{10} \div 3\frac{9}{15}$
14. $2\frac{2}{6} \div 4\frac{2}{3}$
15. $3\frac{1}{2} \div 4\frac{1}{3}$
16. $3\frac{3}{4} \div 1\frac{2}{3}$
17. $9\frac{4}{5} \div 1\frac{4}{10}$
18. $3\frac{1}{5} \div 1\frac{6}{10}$

Dividing Fractions

rewrite / invert and multiply

$$1\frac{2}{3} \div 2\frac{1}{2} = \frac{5}{3} \div \frac{5}{2} = \frac{\cancel{5}}{3} \cdot \frac{2}{\cancel{5}_1} = \frac{2}{3}$$

rewrite

1. $7\frac{4}{5} \div 1\frac{3}{10}$

2. $5\frac{1}{2} \div 8\frac{4}{5}$

3. $9\frac{2}{7} \div 3\frac{3}{14}$

4. $8\frac{2}{5} \div 2\frac{1}{10}$

5. $3\frac{5}{7} \div 3\frac{15}{21}$

6. $8\frac{2}{7} \div 2\frac{1}{14}$

7. $9\frac{1}{6} \div 3\frac{8}{12}$

8. $11\frac{3}{7} \div 5\frac{10}{14}$

9. $7\frac{1}{9} \div 2\frac{2}{3}$

10. $9\frac{3}{5} \div 1\frac{6}{10}$

11. $12\frac{3}{5} \div 2\frac{7}{10}$

12. $8\frac{1}{3} \div 4\frac{1}{6}$

13. $7\frac{1}{2} \div 8\frac{3}{4}$

14. $9\frac{1}{5} \div 2\frac{3}{10}$

15. $12\frac{4}{5} \div 1\frac{1}{15}$

16. $10\frac{4}{5} \div 1\frac{8}{10}$

17. $13\frac{3}{4} \div 5\frac{1}{2}$

18. $3\frac{3}{4} \div 3\frac{1}{8}$

Name______________________________

Fractions Practice

Perform the indicated operation for each pair of fractions below.

1. $5\frac{3}{5} + 8\frac{1}{4}$

2. $15\frac{3}{4} \cdot 3\frac{3}{7}$

3. $12\frac{1}{9} - 7\frac{5}{6}$

4. $7\frac{1}{2} \div 4\frac{1}{6}$

5. $\frac{7}{9} \cdot \frac{3}{14}$

6. $5\frac{5}{8} \cdot 5\frac{1}{3}$

7. $4\frac{2}{5} \div 3\frac{3}{10}$

8. $7\frac{1}{2} + 9\frac{3}{5}$

9. $\frac{3}{5} \div \frac{4}{5}$

10. $11\frac{1}{2} - 2\frac{3}{7}$

11. $15\frac{5}{6} + 3\frac{4}{9}$

12. $9\frac{3}{5} \div 3\frac{6}{10}$

13. $8 - 3\frac{2}{7}$

14. $3\frac{1}{3} \cdot 10\frac{4}{5}$

15. $7\frac{3}{5} + 4\frac{7}{8}$

16. $9\frac{1}{3} \div 2\frac{4}{12}$

17. $4\frac{4}{5} \cdot 3\frac{3}{4}$

18. $4\frac{2}{15} - 1\frac{11}{12}$

19. $4\frac{6}{3} + 6\frac{2}{3}$

20. $6\frac{6}{45} - 2\frac{4}{45}$

21. $8\frac{6}{30} + 6\frac{5}{15}$

Problem Solving With Fractions

A recipe calls for $\frac{3}{4}$ pound of raisins and $\frac{1}{2}$ pound of dates. How many pounds are needed in all? $\frac{3}{4} + \frac{1}{2} = 1\frac{1}{4}$

1. A football team played 27 games and won $\frac{2}{3}$ of them.
How many games did the team win?
How many games did the team lose?

2. A punch recipe calls for $\frac{2}{3}$ cup of apple juice, $\frac{3}{4}$ cup of orange juice, 1 cup of lemon juice, and $\frac{1}{2}$ cup of lime juice. How many cups of juice are needed to make this punch?

3. Evie went to the grocery store to buy some cereal. A one-pound box of cereal costs $2.25. A one-half pound box of cereal costs $1.65. How much money would Evie save if she bought a one-pound box of cereal instead of 2 one-half pound boxes?

4. Delaney wants to make a wedding cake. The recipe calls for $8\frac{1}{2}$ cups of flour. A 16-ounce bag contains 2 cups. How many bags of flour must Delaney buy in order to make her cake?

5. If $2\frac{1}{2}$ pounds of apples cost $2.35 and $2\frac{2}{3}$ pounds of strawberries cost $2.50, which fruit is less expensive per pound?

6. A cookie recipe calls for $1\frac{1}{3}$ cups of flour, $1\frac{2}{3}$ cups of sugar, $2\frac{2}{3}$ cups of raisins, and $3\frac{2}{3}$ cups of walnuts. How many cups of dry ingredients are needed for this recipe?

Changing Fractions to Decimals

$\frac{1}{4} \rightarrow$

```
    .25
4 ) 1.00
     80
     --
     20
     20
     --
      0
```

$\rightarrow \frac{1}{4} = .25$ terminating

$\frac{1}{3} \rightarrow$

```
   .3333
3 ) 1.00
     9
    --
     10
      9
     --
      10
       9
      --
      10
```

$\rightarrow \frac{1}{3} = .\overline{3}$ repeating

Change to decimals.

1. $\frac{3}{4}$

6. $\frac{2}{3}$

11. $\frac{4}{33}$

2. $\frac{6}{16}$

7. $\frac{25}{37}$

12. $\frac{13}{15}$

3. $\frac{18}{22}$

8. $\frac{11}{13}$

13. $\frac{12}{25}$

4. $\frac{5}{16}$

9. $\frac{23}{33}$

14. $\frac{1}{9}$

5. $\frac{7}{15}$

10. $3\frac{1}{4}$

15. $1\frac{3}{5}$

Changing Fractions to Decimals

Change each fraction to a decimal. Do not round the answers.

1. $\frac{6}{9}$	8. $\frac{6}{15}$	15. $\frac{30}{45}$
2. $\frac{19}{57}$	9. $\frac{57}{63}$	16. $\frac{21}{36}$
3. $\frac{10}{70}$	10. $\frac{32}{36}$	17. $\frac{56}{74}$
4. $\frac{13}{39}$	11. $\frac{9}{36}$	18. $\frac{12}{18}$
5. $\frac{8}{24}$	12. $\frac{45}{72}$	19. $\frac{56}{63}$
6. $\frac{6}{21}$	13. $\frac{35}{55}$	20. $\frac{7}{49}$
7. $\frac{6}{39}$	14. $\frac{4}{36}$	21. $\frac{16}{72}$

Rounding Decimals

Round 10.943 to the nearest tenth.
10.943 / 4 < 5 therefore 10.943=10.9

Round 32.78 to the nearest whole number
32.78 / 32.78 / 7 ≥ 5 therefore 32.78=33

Round to the nearest whole number.

1. 42.675	2. 29.78	3. 34.87	4. 21.098
5. 15.91	6. 78.412	7. 7.8346	8. 54.927
9. 2.72	10. 54.909	11. 1.19	12. 4.98

Round to the nearest tenth.

1. 33.897	2. 121.343	3. 32.777	4. 5.345
5. 1.908	6. 341.08	7. 1.23	8. 1.6578
9. 3.869	10. 41.564	11. 654.34	12. 111.111

Round to the nearest hundredth.

1. 212.658	2. 21.569	3. 2.6354	4. 241.560
5. 7.34587	6. 218.453	7. 12.1212	8. 430.234
9. 12.7689	10. 129.404	11. 6.435	12. 9.9999

Multiplying and Dividing by 10, 100, 1000, etc.

23.76 x 1<u>0</u> = 23.76 = 237.6
Move the decimal point to the right one place.

23.76 x 1<u>00</u> = 23.76 = 2376
Move the decimal point to the right two places.

23.765 x 1<u>000</u> = 23.765 = 23765
Move the decimal point to the right three places

237.6 ÷ 1<u>000</u> = 237.6 = .2376
Move the decimal point to the left three places.

Multiply or divide using mental math.

1. 3.456 x 10
2. 345.682 ÷ 100
3. 3.7823 x 1000
4. 5463.23 ÷ 10,000
5. 67,000 ÷ 100
6. .000999 x 1,000
7. 67.009 ÷ 1000
8. 81 x 100
9. 23,098 ÷ 10,000
11. 48.98 x 10,000
12. .092 ÷ 100
13. .0442 x 100,000
14. 4.881 ÷ 100,000
15. 2.785 x 10
16. .0098 ÷ 100
17. 4.342 x 100,000
18. 45,000 ÷ 1000
19. 2.8 x 10
20. .91 ÷ 10,000
21. 32.949 x 100

Adding Decimals

13.3 + 7.23 =	13.30
	+ 7.23
	20.53

Add.

1. 3.456 + 2.894
2. 4.89 + 5.73
3. 3.5 + 8.4
4. 43.56 + 105.7
5. 15.76 + 34.23 + 3.9
6. 6.8 + 13.634 + 2.34
7. 5.7 + 5.34 + 4.78
8. 12.87 + 2.87
9. $13.39 + $7.40
10. .017 + 13
11. 5.02 + 5.20
12. 9.91 + 2.734 + 8.41
13. 121.9 + .736
14. 17.438 + 4.82
15. 322.815 + 6.876
16. 5.97 + 4.87 + 3.908
17. 3.83 + 45.90 + 5.00
18. 5.94 + 5.32
19. 6.41 + 3.99
20. 2.987 + 451.90

Adding Decimals

11.2 + 6.12 =	11.20 + 6.12 17.32

Add.

1. 2.312 + 5.371

2. 3.09 + 2.19

3. 2.15 + 4.58

4. 61.71 + 324.95

5. 46.29 + 22.53 + 5.6

6. 2.6 + 21.540 + 3.65

7. 5.4 + 7.38 + 6.21

8. 27.34 + 6.45

9. \$12.52 + \$8.32

10. .032 + 37

11. 3.43 + 5.45

12. 5.66 + 7.34 + 6.30

13. 281.7 + .736

14. 23.431 + 5.34

15. 654.595 + 3.650

16. 6.29 + 9.95 + 6.332

17. 8.45 + 95.20 + 5.34

18. 5.37 + 7.37

19. 8.22 + 8.41

20. 5.372 + 371.52

Subtracting Decimals

17.2 - 5.10 =

$$\begin{array}{r} 17.20 \\ \underline{-\ 5.10} \\ 12.10 \end{array}$$

Subtract.

1. 13.2 – 6.7
2. 13.3 – 12.4
3. 62.1 – 33.29
4. 76.34 – 47.30
5. 325.34 – 235.34
6. 55.23 – 47.29
7. $21.73 – $16.43
8. 3.239 – .06
9. 23.28 – .002 – 1.2
10. 35.63 – .021
11. 543.43 – 35.342
12. 436.82 – 328.56
13. 75.034 – 22.439
14. 439.02 – 232.76
15. 756.98 – 32.43
16. 65.9 – 33.32
17. 21.32 – 4.28
18. 4.64 – .476
19. 121.32 – 4.34
20. 34.32 – 12.43

Subtracting Decimals

$$13.5 - 4.21 = \begin{array}{r} 13.50 \\ \underline{-\,4.21} \\ 9.29 \end{array}$$

Subtract.

1. 4.7 – 2.3
2. 24.34 – 23.19
3. 84.87 – 78.45
4. 85.76 – 34.65
5. 342.43 – 259.24
6. 74.81 – 61.92
7. $54.68 – $23.76
8. 7.435 – .0345
9. 43.50 – .015 – 3.2
10. 56.40 – .043
11. 756.84 – 31.343
12. 34,245.34 – 28,674.87
13. 82.72 – 43.658
14. 954.34 – 657.56
15. 843.44 – 22.39
16. 84.8 – 44.87
17. 93.76 – 8.67
18. 6.56 – .654
19. 254.54 – 6.45
20. 39.43 – 15.34

Name________________________________ *Decimals*

Multiplying Decimals-Calculator Activities

(.6) (.07)

3 decimal places——— .042

$$\begin{array}{r} .6 \\ \times\ .07 \\ \hline .042 \end{array}$$

Multiply. Use a calculator.

1. (.004) (8)
2. (.051) (.006)
3. (340) (.02)
4. (9.4) (3)
5. (4.52) (6)
6. (3.28) (12.8)
7. (.016) (3.8)
8. (.004) (4) (.04)
9. (1.4) (.978) (.07)
10. (.05) (.17) (.002)
11. (.34) (.12) (.104)
12. (11.9) (.02) (3.09)
13. (12.3) (5.81) (.06)
14. (4) (.112)
15. (12.89) (.331)
16. (3.906) (12.12)
17. (2.09) (.005)
18. (18.92) (.4) (.32)
19. (.012) (6) (.05)
20. (8) (.342) (.02)

Multiplying Decimals

(.4) (.06) — 3 decimal places

$$\begin{array}{r} .4 \\ \times\ .06 \\ \hline .024 \end{array}$$

Multiply. Use mental math

1. 0.06 x 0.4
2. (1.2) (0.03)
3. (0.9) (0.9)
4. 0.03 x 0.08
5. 0.5 x 0.06
6. (0.11) (0.05)
7. (0.7) (0.07)
8. 0.12 x 0.04
9. (0.8) (0.005)
10. (0.9) (0.002)
11. (0.012) (0.7)
12. (0.7) (0.011)
13. 0.03 x 0.6
14. (1.1) (0.11)
15. (0.12) (.05)
16. 0.06 x 0.07
17. (0.10) (0.05)
18. (0.012) (1.2)
19. (0.6) (0.8)
20. (0.02) (1.2)

Dividing Decimals-Calculator Activities

.0173613 ÷ .33 =

$$\begin{array}{r} .05261 \\ 33\overline{)01.73613} \\ \underline{165} \\ 186 \\ \underline{66} \\ 201 \\ \underline{198} \\ 33 \\ \underline{33} \\ 0 \end{array}$$

Divide. Use a calculator.

1. 12.63 ÷ .9
2. 3.56 ÷ 2.5
3. 9.434 ÷ 3.03
4. 42.78 ÷ .187
5. 8.3096 ÷ 5.2
6. 1.35 ÷ .07
7. 12.257 ÷ 5.8
8. 3.908 ÷ 3.2
9. 7.76 ÷ 1.2
10. 6.56 ÷ .16
11. .0135 ÷ 4.5
12. .483 ÷ .22
13. 9.414 ÷ 3.3
14. 16.73 ÷ .12
15. .1927 ÷ .0543
16. 9.54 ÷ 3.03

Dividing Decimals

Divide. Use mental math.

1. $0.36 \div 0.4$
2. $5.4 \div 0.06$
3. $1.21 \div 0.11$
4. $1.69 \div 0.13$
5. $0.032 \div 0.4$
6. $9.6 \div 0.12$
7. $14.4 \div 1.2$
8. $0.012 \div 0.3$
9. $0.56 \div 0.008$
10. $0.072 \div 0.08$
11. $2.6 \div 0.02$
12. $0.55 \div 0.005$
13. $0.0027 \div 0.9$
14. $100 \div 0.01$
15. $0.132 \div 0.012$
16. $7.2 \div 0.06$
17. $0.064 \div 0.8$
18. $0.0054 \div 0.006$
19. $3.6 \div 0.009$
20. $0.24 \div 0.008$
21. $84 \div 1.2$
22. $0.108 \div 0.09$

Practice with Decimals

Perform the indicated operation.

1. 2.62 ÷ .54
2. 31.25 + 23.5
3. (9.9) (2.03)
4. 8726 ÷ 2.84
5. 1.32 ÷ 1.22
6. 6.55 + .08
7. 12.78 – 7.2
8. (3.2) (4.065)
9. 21.7 – 15.9
10. .6 + .09 + 1.75
11. (2.5) (3.4) (4.4)
12. 87.21 –23.98 + 11.12
13. (.03) (.23) (1.3)
14. 23.65 ÷ 22.81
15. 2.34 ÷ .983
16. 65.78 + 54.90
17. 432.42 – 237.89
18. 12.938 + 11.548
19. 789.987 – 231.093
20. (13.2) (34.9)
21. 1243.32 – 1032.90
22. 5.23 ÷ 3.12

Practice with Decimals

Perform the indicated operation.

1. 3.56 ÷ .73
2. 22.59 + 33.5
3. (4.3) (3.59)
4. 3496 ÷ 3.549
5. 7.459 ÷ 2.459
6. 7.546 + .0958
7. 15.54 – 8.34
8. (6.5) (5.304)
9. 43.7 – 34.5
10. .8 + .07 + 3.73
11. (5.5) (2.6) (4.0)
12. 33.54 –22.56 + 23.43
13. (2.3) (3.04) (3.46)
14. 84.34 ÷ 65.76
15. 4.33 ÷ .393
16. 54.34 + 31.98
17. 843.21 – 342.03
18. 23.434 + 23.403
19. 345.765 – 237.405
20. (23.4) (3.9)
21. 1465.65 – 1253.42
22. 6.37 ÷ 6.50

Problem Solving With Decimals

Marilyn and Mackie decided to go the the beach. They went to a grocery store and bought some sandwiches for $5.67, a gallon of fruit punch for $2.31, and a bag of potato chips for $1.21. How much did they spend altogether?

$5.67 + $2.31 + $1.21=

$5.67	each grocery item
$2.31	
+$1.21	
$9.19	total

1. Wilson and Linda went to the dress store to buy Linda a new dress. The dress that Linda picked out costs $95.00. If the price was reduced by $13.68, how much will Linda pay?

2. Norman's credit card bill was $23.43 for January, $65.98 for February, and $21.90 for March. What were his total charges for the first three months of the year?

3. Faith went to her favorite store and bought a sweater for $82.95. She then went to a shoe store and bought a pair of shoes for $87.34. How much money did Faith spend altogether?

4. Lamar loves to go fishing. Before his last trip he decided to buy a few more pieces of equipment. He bought a tackle box for $23.98, a fishing pole for $54.93, a life jacket for $34.21, and an ice chest for $121.28. How much did Lamar spend all together?

5. Nancy and Kathy decided to make a quilt instead of buying one. The materials for the quilt totaled $45.87. The cost of a new quilt is $78.98. How much money did they save?

6. Joann loves to shop. On her last shopping trip she bought a dress for $34.90, a pair of shoes for $89.09, a hat for $65.99, a coat for $34.21, and a belt for $12.99. How much did Joann spend altogether?

Changing Decimals to Fractions

Terminating Decimals	Repeating Decimals
$.50 = \frac{50}{100} = \frac{1}{2}$	$x = .\overline{3} = .3333...$
	$10x = 3.333...$
$.120 = \frac{120}{1000} = \frac{3}{25}$	$-x = 0.333....$
	$9x = 3$
	$x = \frac{1}{3}$
	or $.\overline{3} = \frac{1}{3}$

Express each decimal as a fraction in lowest terms.

1. $.36$
2. $.91\overline{6}$
3. $.625$
4. $.55$
5. $.\overline{46}$
6. $.\overline{33}$
7. $.3\overline{8}$
8. $.775$
9. $.6875$
10. $.5625$
11. $.\overline{27}$
12. $.212$

Changing Decimals to Fractions

Change each decimal to a fraction.

1. $.345$
2. $.1\overline{34}$
3. $.942$
4. $.5\overline{48}$
5. $.438$
6. $.34$
7. $.506$
8. $.65$
9. $.166$
10. $.9\overline{33}$
11. $.229$
12. $.129$
13. $.333$
14. $.243$
15. $.28$
16. $.59$
17. $.342$
18. $.7\overline{34}$
19. $.930$
20. $.777$
21. $.819$
22. $.378$

Percents

Fraction to percent

$\frac{1}{2} \Rightarrow \frac{1}{2} = \frac{x}{100}$

$100 = 2x$

$50 = x$

$\frac{1}{2} = 50\%$

Decimal to percent

$.535 \Rightarrow .535 = 53.5\%$

When converting a decimal to a percent, move the decimal 2 places to the right.

Write each expression as a percent.
Round answers to the nearest hundredth.

1. $\frac{5}{46}$

2. 2.392

3. 2.3838

4. $\frac{7}{15}$

5. 3.293

6. 17.3839

7. 11.6

8. 412.32

9. $\frac{12}{17}$

10. $\frac{11}{23}$

11. 4.34

12. $\frac{4}{13}$

Percents

80%

$80\% = \frac{80}{100} = \frac{8}{10} = \frac{4}{5}$

51.5%

$51.5\% = \frac{51.5}{100} = \frac{515}{1000} = \frac{21}{40}$

Write each percent as a fraction and each fraction as a percent.

1. $4\frac{5}{46}$
2. 8.6%
3. 4.934%
4. $1\frac{1}{4}$
5. .98%
6. 564.89%
7. 12.4%
8. 5.75%
9. 23.7%
10. 21.98%
11. $7\frac{4}{23}$
12. $3\frac{56}{77}$
13. 2.98%
14. $21\frac{7}{32}$
15. $6\frac{1}{2}$
16. $2\frac{5}{7}$

Percents

50% of 40 = ______	____% of 20 = 10	40% of _____ = 20
$\frac{50}{100} = \frac{x}{40}$	$\frac{x}{100} = \frac{10}{20}$	$\frac{40}{100} = \frac{20}{x}$
100x = 2000	20x = 1000	40x = 2000
x = 20	x = 50 50%	x = 50

Solve each percent equation.

1. 20% of 12 = _____
2. 30% of 80 = _____
3. 16% of 85 = _____
4. 17% of 65 = _____
5. 45% of 50 = _____
6. _____% of 25 = 15
7. _____% of 40 = 10
8. _____% of 48 = 8
9. _____% of 65 = 33
10. _____% of 9 = 4
11. 34% of _____ = 34
12. 67% of _____ = 80
13. 20% of _____ = 75
14. 45% of _____ = 120
15. 12% of _____ = 76
16. 60% of _____ = 44

Problems With Percents

A baseball team played 50 games. They won 50% of them. How many games did the team win?

50% of 50 = _____

$$\frac{50}{100} = \frac{x}{50}$$

$$100x = 250$$

$$x = 25$$

1. In a group of 50 children, 18 have red shirts. What percent have red shirts?

2. A test had 80 questions. Diane got 90% of them correct. How many problems did Diane get correct?

3. A soccer team played 32 games. They won 25% of them. how many games did the team win?

4. The regular price of a blouse is $34.00. Find the amount of the discount and the reduced price if there is a 30% discount.

5. A puppy weighed 4.5 pounds at 5 weeks and 7.5 pounds at 8 weeks. What was the percent increase?

6. Sam went to a restaurant and decided to give the waiter a 15% tip. If the bill is $13.50, how much should Sam tip the waiter?

7. John bought a new computer that costs $85.00. The printer is 13% of the purchase price. Find the total cost including the printer.

8. Sugar-free gum contains 40% less calories than regular gum. If a piece of regular gum contains 40 calories, how may calories does a piece of sugar-free gum contain?

Name________________________________

Adding Integers with Like Signs

5 + 6 = 11 (positive)
2 positives

-4 + -11 = -15 (negative)
2 negatives

Find each sum.

1. 5 + 6
2. -12 + -7
3. 32 +53
4. -34 + -76
5. 142 + 374
6. -42 + - 38
7. 45 + 8
8. -61 + -39
9. 23 + 72
10. -17 + -17
11. 90 + 52
12. -13 + -34 + -67
13. 23 + 45 + 65
14. -43 + -36 + -21
15. 13 + 45 + 84
16. -16 + -16 + -16
17. 15 + 41 + 7
18. -2 + -124 + -438
19. 12 + 45 + 396
20. -12 + -37 + -48 + -361

Name________________________________

Adding Integers with Like Signs

7 + 7 = 14 (positive)	-6 + -12 = -18 (negative)
2 positives	2 negatives

Find each sum.

1. 7 + 8
2. -14 + -9
3. 47 +93
4. -21 + -34
5. 213 + 375
6. -163 + -538
7. 28 + 67
8. -12 + -68
9. 34 + 46
10. -23 + -48
11. 70 + 82
12. -21 + -22 + -41
13. 54 + 63 + 82
14. -21 + -41 + -55
15. 36 + 57 + 58
16. -18 + -34 + -59
17. 21 + 22 + 23
18. -21 + -59 + -828
19. 51 + 87 + 527
20. -13 + -67 + -78 + -832

Adding Integers with Unlike Signs

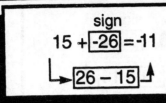

sign
15 + [-26] = -11
└→ [26 – 15] ┘↑

sign
-13 + [27] = 14
└→ [27 – 13] ┘↑

Find each sum.

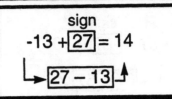

1. 8 + -9
2. -18 + 6
3. 56 + -7
4. -17 + 33
5. -213 + 56
6. -167 + 121
7. 48 + -56
8. -61 + 61
9. 672 + -423
10. -19 + 39
11. -73 + 42
12. 419 + -673
13. -2,895 + 576
14. 17,985 + -33,789
15. 45,908 + -12,921
16. -563,937 + 76,412
17. -12 + 9
18. 46 + -34
19. 57 + -90
20. -87,121 + 86,323

Name________________________________ *Integers*

Adding Integers with Unlike Signs

sign	sign
57 + [-67] = -10 → [67 – 57]	-16 + [29] = 13 → [29 – 16]

Find each sum.

1. 34 + -78
2. -194 + 635
3. 321 + -393
4. -43 + 68
5. -343 + 439
6. -595 + 630
7. 88 + -34
8. -99 + 94
9. 850 + -828
10. -73 + 29
11. -6,907 + 4,262
12. 713 + -6,976
13. -23,895 + 5,863
14. 232,985 + -454,202
15. 67,999 + -78,952
16. -112,956 + 565,453
17. -65,908 + 73,912
18. 57,980 + -41,978
19. 57,908 + -84,512
20. -84,154 + 89,343

Name____

Subtracting Integers

7 – 11 = 7 + -11 = -4 ↑ add the opposite	7 – -11 = 7 + 11 = 18 ↑ add the opposite

Simplify each subtraction expression by "adding the opposite" of the second number.

1. 17 – 26
2. -8 – 5
3. 45 – 23
4. -57 – (-34)
5. -117 – 29
6. 19 – (-342)
7. 232 – 154
8. -8 – (-28)
9. 65 – 85
10. -87 – 129
11. 56 – (-67)
12. -19 – (-13)
13. 78 – 28
14. -749 – 629
15. -594 – (-73)
16. 1,897 – (-492)
17. 9,767 – 2,672
18. 187 – (-48)
19. 677 – 896
20. 897 – (-402)

Name____________________________________

Subtracting Integers

Simplify each subtraction expression by "adding the opposite" of the second number.

1. 7 – 16
2. -18 – 6
3. -45 – (-45)
4. -21 – (-45)
5. -154 – 56
6. 3 – (-26)
7. 0 – 15
8. -3 – (-7)
9. -5 – (-67)
10. -47 – 56
11. -36 – 69
12. -23 – 56
13. -56 – (-95)
14. -60 – 17
15. 319 – (-749)
16. -625 – 117
17. 564 – (-373)
18. 6,793 – (-6,967)
19. -9,774 – 8,834
20. 108,762 – (-95,671)
21. -934 – (-672)
22. -975,834 – (-123,856)
23. -629,905 – (-532,907)
24. 897,342 – (-402,231)

Name______________________________ *Integers*

Adding & Subtracting Integers

Simplify each subtraction expression by "adding the Opposite" of the second number.

1. -8 + -9
2. -10 – 4
3. -15 + 20
4. 31 – (-8)
5. -17 + 9
6. -9 – (-26)
7. -78 – 65
8. 13 + -7
9. 113 – (-62)
10. 0 – (-9)
11. 34 + -68
12. 608 – 343
13. -24 – (-38)
14. 0 – 17
15. -56 – 45
16. 73 + -18
17. -232 – (-232)
18. -108 + -676
19. 43 + -56 – 78
20. -98 – (-126) + 19
21. 91 – 176 – (-11)
22. -17 + 436 + -642
23. -121 + -732 – (-13)
24. -534 – (-454) + -78

Multiplying Integers

Like signs–Positive		Unlike signs–Negative	
(3) (2) = 6	(-2) (-4) = 8	(-3) (2) = -6	(2) (-4) = 8
+ • + = +	- • - = +	- • + = -	+ • - = -

Multiply.

1. (-3) (9)
2. (15) (-4)
3. (35) (3)
4. (32) (-48)
5. (56) (12)
6. (-76) (43)
7. (-39) (-58)
8. (-323) (-10)
9. (37) (-90)
10. (-11) (-11)
11. (-19) (-10) (2) (3)
12. (-5) (-28) (-23)
13. (12) (-28)
14. (33) (-123) (12)
15. (14) (-33) (2)
16. (20) (-3) (23) (-3)
17. (12) (-12) (2) (-44)
18. (121) (-10) (21)
19. (-9) (-88) (-7)
20. (-32) (-33) (-34)

Name________________________________

Multiplying Integers

(4) (5) = 20   (-4) (-1) =4

+ • + = +   - • - = +

Like signs–Positive

(-1) (2) = -2   (8) (-3)=-24

- • + = -   + • - = -

Unlike signs–Negative

Multiply.

1. (5) (-4) (-2)
2. (-8) (-9)
3. (-7) (-3)
4. (-12) (-5) (-3)
5. (-6) (-2) (-5)
6. (-29) (-2)
7. (21) (-22)
8. (43) (111) (-1)
9. (-5) (-100) (-302)
10. (-66) (213)
11. (-9) (-88) (-7)
12. (-2) (-14) (-4)
13. (-6) (-9)
14. (8) (-103) (-77) (-22)
15. (-7) (-14) (121)
16. (-1) (22) (-33) (44)
17. (-85) (-219)
18. (213) (4) (18)
19. (-19) (-38) (-26)
20. (1) (-42) (-6)

Dividing Integers

$\frac{-27}{-9} = 3$ Like signs = Positive

$49 \div -6 = -8$ Unlike signs = negative

Divide.

1. $200 \div -4$
2. $-60 \div 3$
3. $120 \div -6$
4. $84 \div -21$
5. $-188 \div 4$
6. $144 \div -12$
7. $80 \div -5$
8. $72 \div 4$
9. $-36 \div 6$
10. $-150 \div 6$
11. $\frac{-18}{-18}$
12. $\frac{-104}{8}$
13. $\frac{27}{-9}$
14. $\frac{-77}{7}$
15. $\frac{147}{21}$
16. $\frac{-50}{-5}$
17. $\frac{220}{-10}$
18. $\frac{168}{-14}$
19. $\frac{-288}{-12}$
20. $\frac{-30}{3}$

Name____________________________________ *Integers*

Dividing Integers

Divide.

1. $-13 \div 13$
2. $60 \div -10$
3. $-72 \div 9$
4. $-160 \div -40$
5. $-150 \div 6$
6. $-130 \div -65$
7. $-54 \div -9$
8. $-147 \div -21$
9. $75 \div -3$
10. $-125 \div 5$
11. $-90 \div 2$
12. $-210 \div -5$
13. $\frac{-66}{-11}$
14. $\frac{-655}{-5}$
15. $\frac{-80}{10}$
16. $\frac{-72}{8}$
17. $\frac{-35}{-7}$
18. $\frac{-468}{26}$
19. $\frac{-253}{11}$
20. $\frac{66}{-2}$
21. $\frac{-84}{-7}$
22. $\frac{258}{-3}$
23. $\frac{-310}{5}$
24. $\frac{-552}{23}$

Mixed Practice with Integers

Perform the indicated operations.

1. -34 + -122
2. 80 – (-22)
3. -3 • 5
4. 19 • -23
5. 83 + -85
6. 28 – (-65)
7. 28 – (-26)
8. -31 – (-21)
9. -35 + 62 + -90
10. 12 • -13 • 6
11. (212 + -234 – 222) ÷ -6
12. 100 • 3 • 21
13. $\frac{175}{-5} \bullet -4$
14. $\frac{-555}{-5} \bullet -6$
15. $\frac{-424}{4}$
16. $\frac{-72}{8} + \frac{-64}{8} + \frac{33}{-11}$
17. (225 ÷ 5) • .2
18. (-19 – (-21) – (-34)) ÷ -6
19. (-18 – -77 – 22) • 2
20. (10 + -31 + -80) ÷ 3
21. (16 – 21 + 34) ÷ -8
22. (-320 + -75 + 24) • 4
23. (-12 + 13 + 55) • 3
24. (-12 – 54 – 10) • 2

Problem Solving With Integers

1. A helicopter started at 0 feet. At take off it rose 2100 feet. It then descended 600 feet because the pilot wanted to take a photograph. A flock of birds was approaching so the helicopter rose 3200 feet. After the approaching flock of birds passed, the helicopter descended 2600 feet. How high was the helicopter flying after the last descent?

2. Cindy goes to school in a 7-story building. Her first class is on the first floor. She goes up 3 floors for her second class and down 2 floors for her third class. For her fourth class Cindy goes up 5 floors and for her final class Cindy goes down 1 floor. What floor is Cindy on during her final class?

3. Some number added to -12 is 36. Add this number to -15. Then multiply this number by -2. What is the final number?

4. Some number subtracted by -6 is 41. Multiply this number by -3. Then divide this number by -4. What is the final number?

5. A bus driver started her day with an empty bus. At her first stop she picked up 11 people. At her second stop she picked up 5 more people and let 7 people get off. At her third stop she picked up 5 people and let 2 off. How many people were on the bus as the driver left the third stop?

6. Some number added to -13 is 44. Divide this number by 2. Then multiply by 8. What is the final number?

7. Jim got a job at a ski resort. He was in charge of determining how deep the snow was. On the first day of the snow season it snowed 1 meter. The next day was warmer and .5 meter of the snow melted. On the third day it snowed 2 meters in the morning but by noon 1 meter had melted. How deep was the snow at noon?

8. The library started the year with 14,341 books. At the end of the first week 1456 books had been checked out. At the end of the second week 3,298 books had been checked out and 2,192 books had been returned. How many books were in the library at the end of the second week?

Adding and Subtracting Real Numbers

$-4 + -2 + 2\frac{1}{2} = -6 + 2\frac{1}{2} = -5\frac{2}{2} + 2\frac{1}{2} = -3\frac{1}{2}$

Add or subtract as indicated.

1. $5\frac{1}{5} + -4.34 - 6\frac{1}{3}$
2. $-2 + 6\frac{1}{5} + -4\frac{1}{3}$
3. $-1\frac{2}{3} + -6\frac{5}{11} + 7\frac{2}{3}$
4. $5\frac{5}{12} + -6.44 - 14.69$
5. $-1 + -2\frac{1}{3} + -7\frac{3}{5}$
6. $2\frac{5}{7} - -3\frac{6}{9} + \frac{1}{8}$
7. $17 - 12.2 + -9\frac{2}{5}$
8. $13.23 - -31.73$
9. $12.52 - -7\frac{2}{3} + 18\frac{1}{4}$
10. $7\frac{1}{7} - -9.33 + 7\frac{4}{7}$
11. $-6 - 2\frac{3}{5} + -7\frac{2}{5}$
12. $-5\frac{2}{3} - -6\frac{1}{5} + 1\frac{7}{12}$
13. $7\frac{4}{13} + -9.21 - 16.32$
14. $-3 + -3\frac{1}{4} - -3\frac{3}{7}$
15. $5\frac{5}{8} - -9\frac{2}{3} - \frac{2}{9}$
16. $12 + 13.3 + -9\frac{1}{6}$
17. $4.38 + -4.38$
18. $17.65 + -8\frac{1}{7} + 19\frac{5}{9}$

Adding and Subtracting Real Numbers

Add or subtract indicated operations.

1. $3\frac{2}{3} + -2.25 - 7\frac{2}{4}$

2. $-6 - 7\frac{3}{4} + -2\frac{2}{3}$

3. $-8\frac{1}{2} + -2\frac{4}{12} - 8\frac{1}{3}$

4. $6\frac{1}{10} + -3.25 - 12.65$

5. $-2 - -3\frac{1}{8} + -4\frac{3}{4}$

6. $7\frac{2}{3} - -1\frac{2}{3} + \frac{2}{3}$

7. $12 - 17.3 + -3\frac{2}{3}$

8. $-11.08 - -12.67$

9. $19.22 - -5\frac{3}{4} + 13\frac{2}{3}$

10. $13\frac{2}{5} - 17.8 + 13\frac{4}{5}$

11. $3\frac{7}{10} + -4.23 - 7\frac{3}{8}$

12. $5\frac{2}{7} + -3.43 - 8\frac{3}{11}$

13. $-8 - 1\frac{3}{5} + -6\frac{1}{8}$

14. $-2\frac{3}{7} + -9\frac{6}{10} - 5\frac{2}{3}$

15. $3\frac{1}{15} + -4.38 - 13.47$

16. $-5 - -7\frac{3}{7} + -2\frac{5}{8}$

17. $3\frac{1}{2} - -6\frac{1}{3} - \frac{3}{5}$

18. $17 - 12.2 - -8\frac{4}{9}$

19. $-5.23 + 3.33$

20. $11.62 + -8\frac{6}{7} - 18\frac{1}{9}$

21. $17\frac{8}{9} - 12.2 + 16\frac{2}{7}$

22. $9\frac{2}{3} - -5.61 - 9\frac{1}{5}$

Multiplying and Dividing Real Numbers

$$3 \cdot 6 \cdot \frac{1}{3} = 18 \cdot \frac{1}{3} = \frac{\overset{6}{\cancel{18}}}{1} \cdot \frac{1}{\underset{1}{\cancel{3}}} = 6$$

$$2\frac{1}{3} \cdot 1\frac{3}{4} \div 1\frac{1}{2} = \frac{7}{3} \cdot \frac{7}{4} \div \frac{3}{2} = \frac{7}{3} \cdot \frac{7}{\underset{2}{\cancel{4}}} \cdot \frac{\overset{1}{\cancel{2}}}{3} = \frac{98}{9} \text{ or } 10\frac{8}{9}$$

Multiply or divide as indicated.

1. $2\frac{2}{3} \cdot -6\frac{1}{5}$
2. $-4 \cdot 2\frac{1}{5} \cdot -7\frac{1}{3}$
3. $-9\frac{2}{3} \cdot 3\frac{7}{12}$
4. $1\frac{5}{12} \cdot 3.29$
5. $4 \cdot -2\frac{1}{3} \cdot 2$
6. $5\frac{1}{2} \div -3\frac{1}{6}$
7. $10 \div 2.5 \cdot -1\frac{2}{5}$
8. $3.6 \cdot -31.73$
9. $10.8 \div -2\frac{1}{2} \cdot 3\frac{1}{4}$
10. $2\frac{1}{7} \div -6.22$
11. $-6.3 \cdot 2 \cdot \frac{1}{2}$
12. $5\frac{1}{3} \cdot 9.80 \cdot 0$
13. $11 \cdot 4\frac{1}{12} \cdot -3$
14. $(-3\frac{1}{4})(-3\frac{1}{4}) \div .4$
15. $3\frac{1}{3} \div 1\frac{1}{2} \div \frac{5}{6}$
16. $10 \cdot 12.1 \cdot -6\frac{1}{6}$
17. $7.21 \cdot -2.37$
18. $11.21 \cdot -7\frac{1}{3} \div 22\frac{5}{9}$

Multiplying and Dividing Real Numbers

Multiply or divide as indicated.

1. $1\frac{1}{14} \bullet -3\frac{2}{7}$

2. $-6 \bullet 8\frac{2}{8} \bullet -1\frac{1}{4}$

3. $-5\frac{1}{6} \bullet 2\frac{7}{18}$

4. $3\frac{3}{8} \bullet 2.27$

5. $2 \bullet -1\frac{1}{2} \bullet 5$

6. $3\frac{2}{3} \div -6\frac{1}{5}$

7. $12 \div 2.2 \bullet -4\frac{4}{7}$

8. $4.2 \bullet -12.12$

9. $14.2 \div -6\frac{1}{5} \bullet 2\frac{2}{5}$

10. $13.5 \div -3\frac{2}{3} \bullet 6\frac{3}{7}$

1. $12.8 \div -5\frac{2}{3} \bullet 2\frac{4}{5}$

12. $5\frac{2}{5} \div -3.84$

13. $-2.2 \bullet 5 \bullet \frac{1}{7}$

14. $6\frac{1}{5} \bullet 3.55 \bullet 0$

15. $13 \bullet 5\frac{1}{10} \bullet -2$

16. $(-7\frac{2}{8})(-3\frac{2}{8}) \div .2$

17. $2\frac{1}{5} \div 6\frac{3}{7} \div \frac{4}{6}$

18. $12 \bullet 13.3 \bullet -6\frac{1}{2}$

19. $5.25 \bullet -3.89$

20. $13.26 \bullet -8\frac{1}{3} \div 12\frac{5}{7}$

21. $10.10 \bullet -5\frac{1}{6} \div 20\frac{5}{6}$

22. $13.13 \bullet -13\frac{2}{6} \div 13\frac{1}{3}$

Order of Operations with Real Numbers

$-4 \bullet 3 + 2 = -12 + 2 = -14$

$2\frac{1}{3} \div (4 + 8) = \frac{7}{3} \div 12 = \frac{7}{3} \bullet \frac{1}{12} = \frac{7}{36}$

Perform the indicated operations using order of operations rules.

1. $-25 \div 6 + 4\frac{1}{5}$

2. $\frac{2}{3}(-15 - 4)$

3. $-8 \div -2 + 5 \bullet - \frac{1}{2} - 25 \div 5$

4. $\frac{1}{2}\ [(-15 + 4) + (6 + 7) \div -3]$

5. $(9\frac{1}{3} + 4\frac{1}{3}) \div 6 - -12$

6. $\frac{(80 \div 4) + 25}{-12 + 35}$

7. $3\ [-3\ (2-10) - 5]$

8. $2 \bullet 3\ [5 + (4 \div 2)]$

9. $40 \div [(3 \bullet 3) - (36 \div 9)] + -81$

Order of Operations with Real Numbers

Perform the indicated operations using order of operations rules.

1. $-20 \div 3 + 2\frac{2}{3}$

2. $\frac{1}{4}(-12 + 6)$

3. $-5 \div -3 - 2 \bullet -\frac{1}{3} - 21 \div 7$

4. $\frac{1}{2}[(-12 - 2) + (1 + 8) \div -8]$

5. $(5\frac{1}{5} - 2\frac{1}{5}) \bullet 6 - -16$

6. $\dfrac{(20 \div 2) + 10}{-10 + 20 + 30}$

7. $2[-5(4 - 12) - 3]$

8. $4 \bullet 4[2 - (6 \div 3)]$

9. $20 \bullet [(3 \bullet 6) - (24 \div 8)] + -32$

10. $2 \div [(4 \div 2) + (32 \div 8)]$

11. $[(2 \bullet 2) - (30 \div 6)] + -25 - 23$

Comparing Real Numbers

4.66	______	4.78	$4\frac{1}{2}$	______	4.78
4.66	<	4.78	4.50	<	4.78

Use <, >, or = to make each a true sentence.

1. 2.5 ________ $2\frac{1}{2}$
2. 1.078 ______ 1.78
3. 13.26 _______ 132.6
4. 983.21_______ 7551.7
5. 232.33 _______ 23.233
6. -.3 ________ $-.\overline{3}$
7. $-9\frac{36}{48}$ _______ -9.77
8. $12\frac{5}{8}$ _______ 12.6
9. 1.5 ________ $1\frac{2}{3}$
10. 3.2 ________ $3\frac{1}{5}$

Rewrite any fractions as decimals, then put the decimals for each problem in order from least to greatest.

$2\frac{1}{2}$, $2\frac{3}{5}$, 2.4	2.4, $2\frac{1}{2}$, $2\frac{3}{5}$	2.4, 2.5, 2.6

1. 2.51, 2.511, 2.5111
2. $-3\frac{1}{5}$, $-3\frac{2}{3}$, $-3\frac{5}{7}$
3. $-2\frac{1}{4}$, $2\frac{7}{8}$, $2\frac{3}{9}$
4. $4\frac{2}{3}$, $-4\frac{6}{9}$, 4.34
5. $-6\frac{1}{5}$, -6.66, $-6\frac{4}{5}$
6. 10.78, 10.781, 10.710
7. $5\frac{1}{2}$, $5\frac{1}{3}$, $5\frac{3}{4}$
8. $-1\frac{4}{5}$, $-1\frac{9}{10}$, $-1\frac{7}{8}$
9. $7\frac{2}{3}$, 7.45 , $7\frac{3}{5}$
10. 3.15 , 3.8 , $3\frac{2}{5}$

Open Sentences

$\frac{1}{5} \bullet 10 = x$

$\frac{1}{\cancel{5}_1} \bullet \frac{\cancel{10}^2}{1} = x$

$2 = x$

$\frac{81}{9} - 12 = t$

$9 - 12 = t$

$-3 = t$

Evaluate each expression for the given value of the variable.

1. $\frac{15 + -7}{2} = r$

2. $\frac{11 + 3}{7} = j$

3. $\frac{2 + -18}{4} = p$

4. $\frac{1}{5} \bullet -12 + -9 = w$

5. $-7.5 \bullet 3.3 + 13 = g$

6. $1\frac{3}{5} \div \frac{15}{45} = f$

7. $4 \bullet 3.61 - 16.8 = n$

8. $\frac{-25 + 12}{3} + 6 = b$

9. $-\frac{2}{5} \div \frac{1}{15} + -3\frac{1}{3} = y$

10. $\frac{6 - 12}{3} + 4 = p$

11. $\frac{2}{6} \bullet 13 - 6 = m$

12. $4.34 + 2.22 \div 3 = q$

13. $-2 \bullet 5 - 6 = d$

14. $1 + 2.78 - 6.5 = z$

Open Sentences

$26 = r \bullet 2$, if $r = 13$
$26 = 13 \bullet 2$
$26 = 26$ True

Evaluate each expression for the given value of the variable.

1. $6 + x = 3\frac{1}{3}$, if $= -3\frac{1}{2}$
2. $2 + y = 9$, if $y = 6$
3. $\frac{m}{6} + -4 = 0$, if $m = 6$
4. $y(6 + 3) + 2 = 37$, if $y = 26$
5. $11.2 + .2 - r = 14.1$, if $r = 3.2$
6. $3x + 12 = 15$, if $x = -1$
7. $f(2 + 3) + 1 = 22$, if $f = 16$
8. $\frac{15 + 12}{b} + 6 = 15$, if $b = 3$
9. $-\frac{2}{5} \div \frac{1}{15} + c\ \frac{1}{3} = -3$, if $c = 2$
10. $7 + (e - 31) = -12$, if $e = -12$
11. $\frac{2}{6} \bullet 13 - k = 7$, if $k = 6$
12. $r + 6.32 \div 3 = 2.2$, if $r = -3$
13. $-t \bullet 5 - 6 = -23$, if $t = 5$
14. $z + 13 \div 6.5 = 7$, if $z = -3$

Solving Division Equations

$$\frac{x}{2} = 8$$

$$2 \bullet \frac{x}{2} = 8 \bullet 2$$

$$x = 16$$

Solve each equation for the given variable.

1. $-15 = \frac{x}{3}$

2. $\frac{u}{4} = -36$

3. $\frac{2}{3}c = -8$

4. $.9 = \frac{k}{81}$

5. $\frac{m}{6} = 36$

6. $\frac{1}{12}c = .6$

7. $\frac{1}{7}n = -28$

8. $-12 = \frac{t}{4}$

9. $\frac{x}{4.1} = 16$

10. $\frac{r}{17} = -23$

11. $-3 = \frac{1}{3}x$

12. $\frac{x}{8} = 56$

13. $\frac{3}{7}h = 4.5$

14. $\frac{2}{3}z = 33$

Solving Multiplication and Division Equations

$$4y = -28$$
$$4y \div 4 = -28 \div 4$$
$$1y = -7$$
$$y = -7$$

$$\frac{n}{3} = 9$$
$$3 \bullet \frac{n}{3} = 9 \bullet 3$$
$$n = 27$$

Solve each equation for the given variable.

1. $5n = -75$

2. $12a = 144$

3. $-12r = 12$

4. $49 = -9u$

5. $4.5 = 9y$

6. $3.7 = -.21w$

7. $2\frac{3}{5} = 6c$

8. $-33 = \frac{t}{11}$

9. $\frac{f}{3.6} = 16$

10. $\frac{2}{12}b = -12$

11. $-6 = \frac{x}{6}$

12. $\frac{h}{9} = 63$

13. $\frac{2}{3}c = 5.9$

14. $\frac{1}{5}m = 22$

Solving Equations with 2 Operations

$$3y - 6 = 30$$
$$3y - 6 + 6 = 30 + 6$$
$$3y = 36$$
$$\frac{3y}{3} = \frac{36}{3}$$
$$y = 12$$

Solve each equation for the given variable. Express each answer in lowest terms.

1. $-8r - 7 = -24$
2. $5x - 5 = -10$
3. $9 = 3y + 5$
4. $12 = 6c - 4$
5. $-23 = 3e - (-9)$
6. $16 = -2v + 9$
7. $\frac{3y}{4} = 12$
8. $13n - 13 = -12$
9. $23x - 12 = -33$
10. $-42 = 6b + 8$
11. $16 + 4y = -32$
12. $16 + \frac{r}{2} = -11$
13. $2x - 5 = 16$
14. $11 = 3y - 10$

Name______________________________ *Equations*

Solving Equations Using the Distributive Property

$$3(c - 4) = 15$$
$$3c - 12 = 15$$
$$3c - 12 + 12 = 15 + 12$$
$$\frac{3c}{3} = \frac{27}{3}$$
$$c = 9$$

Solve each equation for the given variable.

1. $3(C + 4) = -7$
2. $35 = -7(z + 3)$
3. $-7(t - 7) = -14$
4. $30 = 5\left(\frac{r}{5} - 3\right)$
5. $16(x - 3) = -33$
6. $36 = 6(x - 5)$
7. $5\left(3 - \frac{c}{7}\right) = 8$
8. $2(n + 6) = 80$
9. $3(8 - 6n) = 41$
10. $7(2x-3) + 3 = 24$
11. $2(9x - 8) = -22$
12. $-36 = 2(x + 4)$
13. $-4(6 + n) + 3 = 38$
14. $-23 = 5(t - 4)$

Solving Equations

$$3x + 5 = 4x + 6$$
$$3x - 4x + 5 = 4x - 4x + 6$$
$$-x + 5 = 6$$
$$-x + 5 - 5 = 6 - 5$$
$$-x = 1$$
$$\frac{-x}{-1} = \frac{1}{-1}$$
$$x = -1$$

Solve each equation for the given variable.

1. $3m - 8 = 5m + 8$
2. $-t + 9 = t + 5$
3. $7y - 7 = 5y + 13$
4. $4h + 10 = 2h - 22$
5. $-r - 3 = 1 - 3r$
6. $17 + p = 7p - 13$
7. $4x - 7 = 2x + 7$
8. $23b + 9 = 4b + 66$
9. $-4g + 12 = g + 2$
10. $-8t = 27 + t$
11. $13y - 26 = 7y + 22$
12. $4n - 6 = 6n + 14$
13. $e + 8 = 2e - 12$
14. $9w + 6 = 6w - 15$

Name____________________________________ *Equations*

Solving equation / Mixed Practice

Solve each equation for the given variable.

1. $-j + 5 = j - 7$

2. $9w + 9 = 3w - 15$

3. $3g + 12 = 6g - 3$

4. $45 = -9(e + 8)$

5. $4(y - 8) = -12$

6. $24 = 4\left(\frac{h}{2} - 7\right)$

7. $11g = 121$

8. $-13k = 52$

9. $35 = -7t$

10. $3h + 5 = 2h - 9$

11. $6u = 21 - u$

12. $12k + 13 = 8k + 33$

13. $7(9 - 6j) = -63$

14. $-6(36 - 10b) + 8 = 32$

15. $9(8c - 9) = -351$

16. $\frac{m}{2.5} = 22$

17. $\frac{2}{5}h = -20$

18. $-5 = \frac{b}{5}$

Name______________________________ *Problem Solving*

Writing Algebraic Expressions

Three times a number decreased by 7	$3x - 7$
A number increased by 9	$x + 9$
The number divided by 3	$b \div 3$ or $\frac{b}{3}$
The product of 3 and 8	$3 \bullet 8$

1. Eleven times the sum of a number and five times the number

2. Seven times the sum of twice a number and sixteen

3. Eleven times a number decreased by three

ber minus seven

'erence between x and 5

er plus six times the number

d by three times the number

umber and five decreased by two

umber increased by six

of a number and eight

even times a number

nd a number increased by six

Writing Algebraic Expressions

Three times a number decreased by 7	$3x - 7$
A number increased by 9	$x + 9$
A number divided by 3	$b \div 3$ or $\frac{b}{3}$
The product of 3 and 8	$3 \cdot 8$

1. Two-thirds of a number and eight
2. Nine more than the quotient of b and 4
3. Two times the sum of a number and twelve
4. Four-sevenths of a number minus six
5. Three times a number plus five times the number
6. Seven times the difference between c and 4
7. A number increased by four times the number
8. The quotient of a number and four increased by three
9. Two-thirds times a number increased by five
10. Two times a number and eight
11. Three increased by two times a number
12. The quotient of five and a number increased by two

Writing Algebraic Expressions

Write an equation for each and solve.

Nine more than a number is 35. Find the number.

$$9 + x = 35$$

$$9 - 9 + x = 35 - 9$$

$$x = 26$$

1. A number increased by 7 is -23. Find the number.

2. One-third of a number is -20. Find the number.

3. The product of -7 and a number is 35. Find the number.

4. Three times a number is 21. Find the number.

5. The cost of five cakes is $41.00. What is the cost of each cake?

6. The cost of a saddle is $231.00. What is the cost of four saddles?

7. Four times a number is 52. Find the number.

Writing Algebraic Expressions

Write an equation for each and solve.

Eight more than a number is 28. Find the number.

$$8 + x = 28$$

$$8 - 8 + x = 28 - 8$$

$$x = 20$$

1. A number increased by 9 is 41. Find the number.

2. One-fourth of a number is 12. Find the number.

3. The product of -4 and a number is 36. Find the number.

4. Three times a number is 45. Find the number.

5. The cost of five boxes is $22.00. What is the cost of each box?

6. The cost of a television is $432.00. What is the cost of four televisions?

7. Four times a number is 48. Find the number.

Name________________________________

Writing Algebraic Expressions

Write an equation for each and solve.

> Six more than 3 times a number is 21.
> What is the number?
>
> $$6 + 3x = 21$$
> $$6 - 6 + 3x = 21 - 6$$
> $$3x = 15$$
> $$x = 5$$

1. Two-thirds of a number increased by two is ten. What is the number?

2. Six more than a number is negative thirty-one. What is the number?

3. Nine less than three times a number is twenty-seven. What is the number?

4. Two times the sum of a number and five is twenty-six. What is the number?

5. The product of a number and four increased by seven is three. What is the number?

6. The quotient of a number and three decreased by six is two. What is the number?

7. Two more than five times a number is thirty-two. What is the number?

Writing Algebraic Expressions

Write an equation for each and solve for the variable.

> **One number plus 5 times that number equals 120. Find the number.**
>
> $$x + 5x = 120$$
> $$6x = 120$$
> $$x = 20$$

1. **One number plus six times that number equals 133. Find the number.**

2. **The sum of two numbers is 36. The larger number is twice the smaller number. Find the number.**

3. **One number plus three times that number is 44. Find the number.**

4. **The difference between two numbers is 16. The first number is five times the second number. Find the number.**

5. **One number is seven times a second number. Four times the smaller number plus twice the larger number equals 36. Find the number.**

6. **There were 474 tickets sold for the school football game. Students bought five times as many tickets as the faculty did. Find the number of student and faculty tickets sold.**

7. **The sum of two numbers is 126. The larger number is 5 times larger than the smaller number. Find the number.**

Writing Algebraic Expressions

Write an equation for each and solve.

> Seven times a number equals fifteen less than two times the number. Find the number.
>
> $$7x = 2x - 15$$
> $$7x - 2x = 2x - 2x - 15$$
> $$5x = -15$$
> $$x = -3$$

1. One half of a number is 12 more than 2 times the number. Find the number.

2. Thirty decreased by three times a number is six less than three times the number. Find the number.

3. Fifty increased by five times a number is six less than four times the number. Find the number.

4. Twice a number decreased by 39 is five times the sum of the number and two times the number. Find the number.

5. Twelve increased by six times a number is six less than seven times the number. Find the number.

6. Nineteen increased by three times a number is four less than four times the number. Find the number.

7. Four times the sum of a number and three is seven times the number decreased by 3. Find the number.

Number Lines

$s \geq 4$

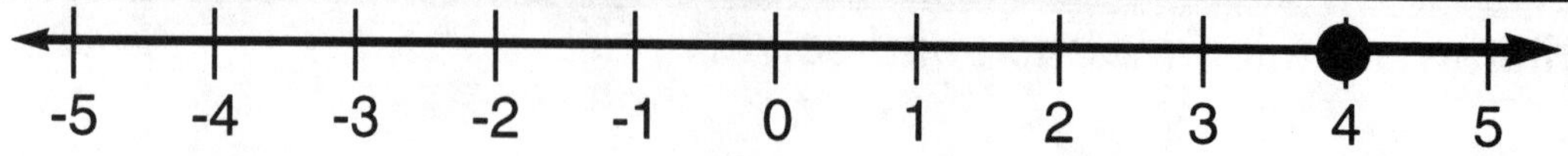

$b \geq 2$

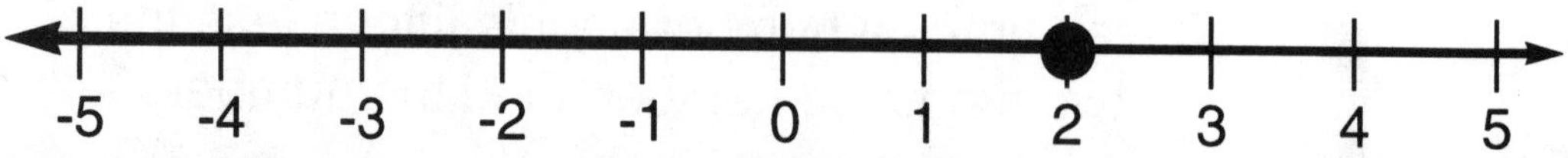

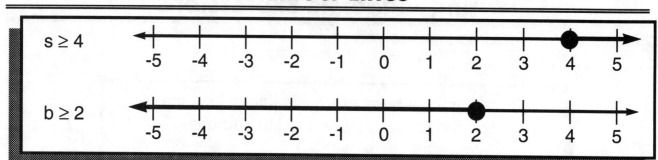

Graph each inequality on the number line.

1. $a > 3$

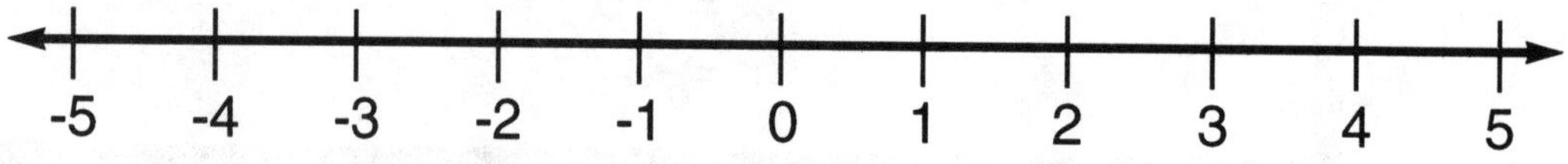

2. $b > -2$

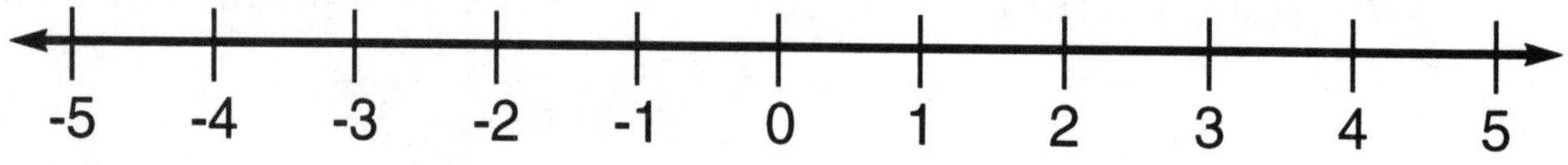

3. $w \geq 3$

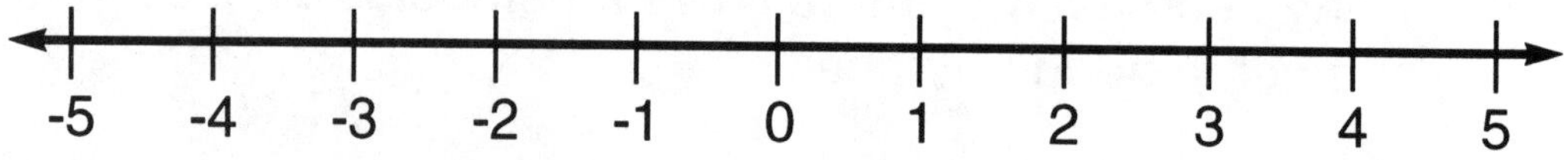

4. $k \leq -2$

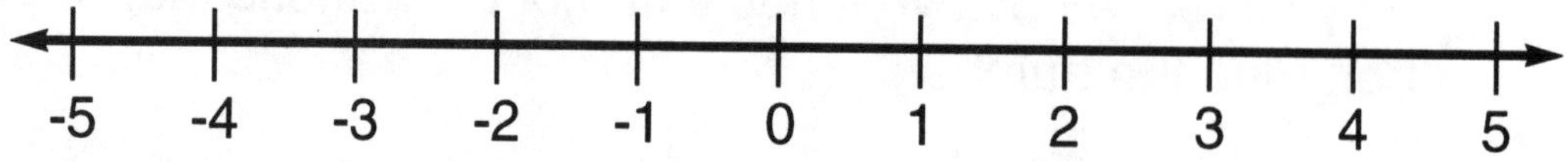

5. $n \geq -2$

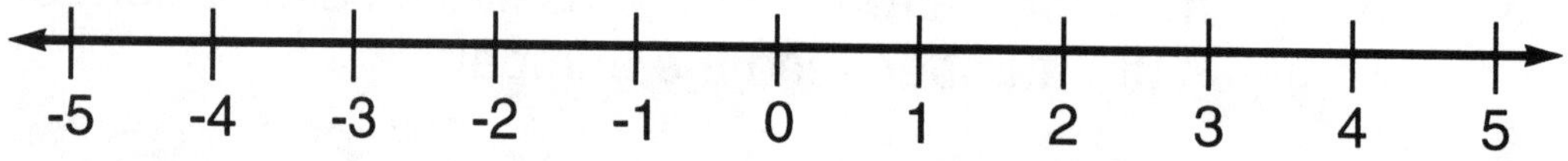

6. $y \leq 4$

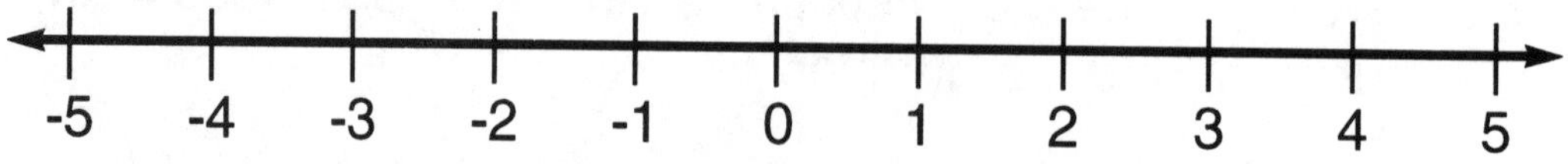

7. $r > \frac{2}{3}$

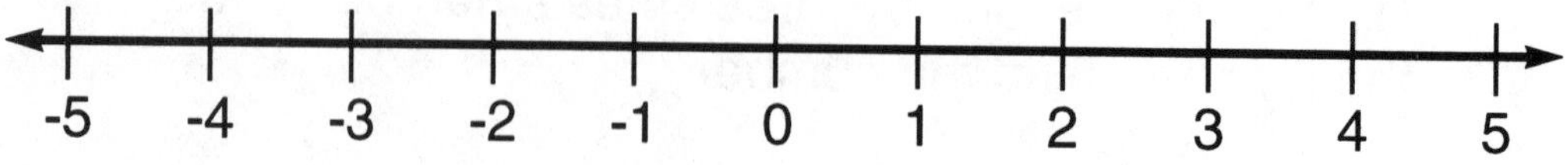

8. $x \geq -\frac{1}{2}$

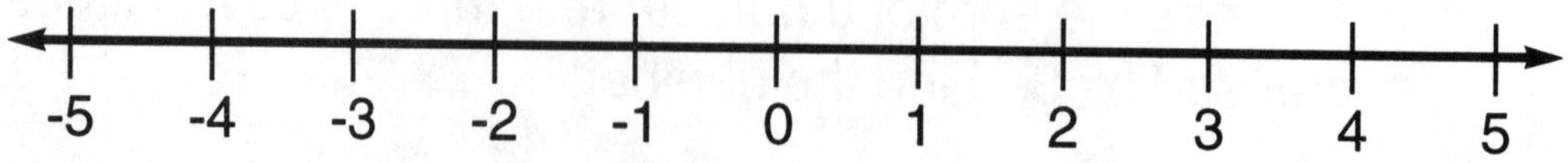

Solving Inequalities with Addition and Subtraction

$$x + 7 < 6$$
$$x + 7 - 7 < 6 - 7$$
$$x < -1$$

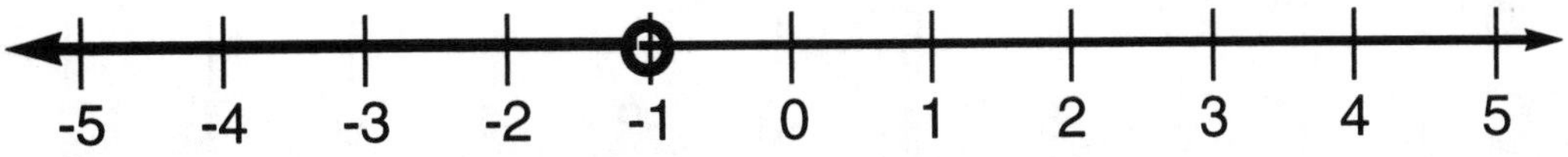

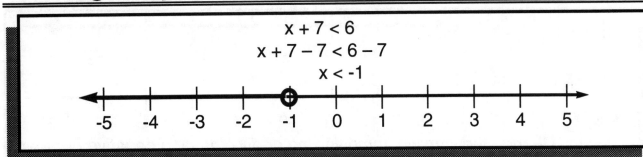

Solve each inequality and graph on the number line.

1. $1 > 3 - d$

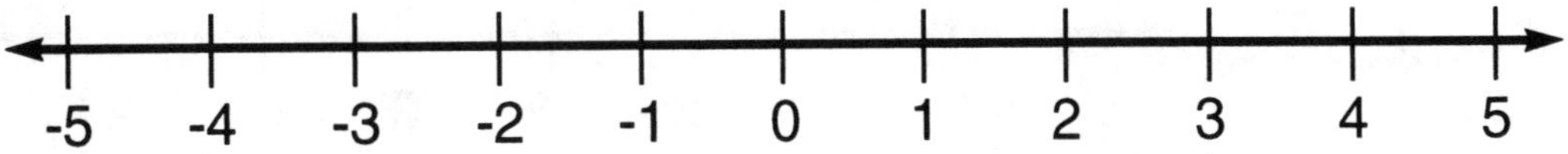

2. $f - 4 > -2$

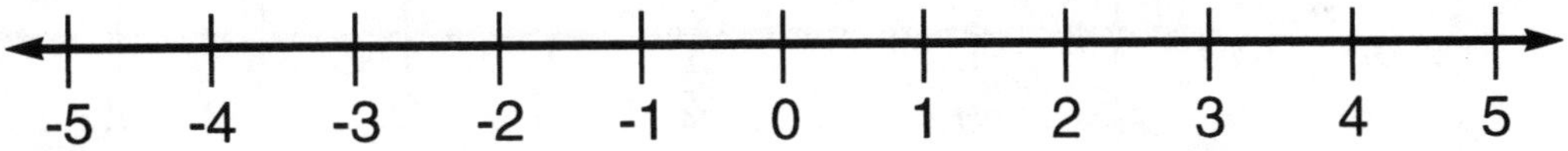

3. $2 > y + 2$

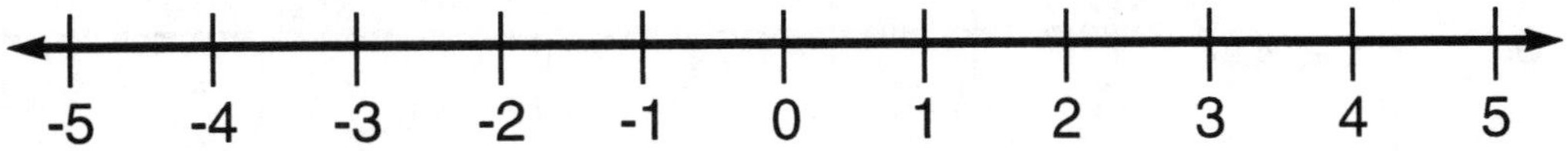

4. $x - 4 \leq 2$

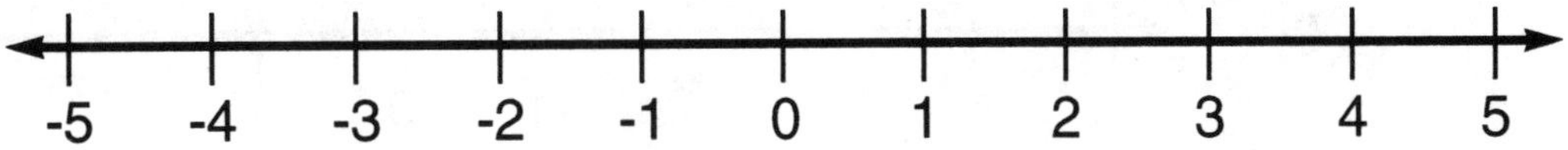

5. $-3 \leq 2 + g$

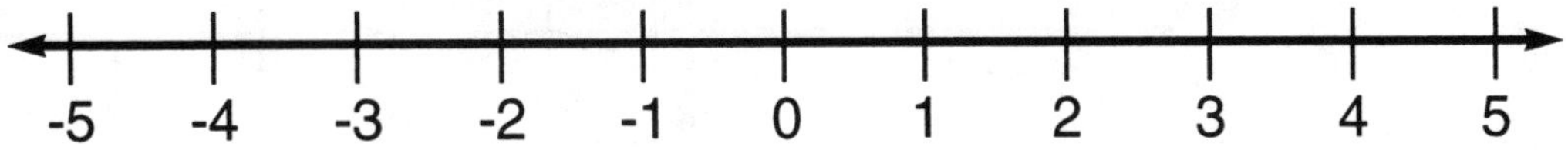

6. $2.3 \geq s + 3$

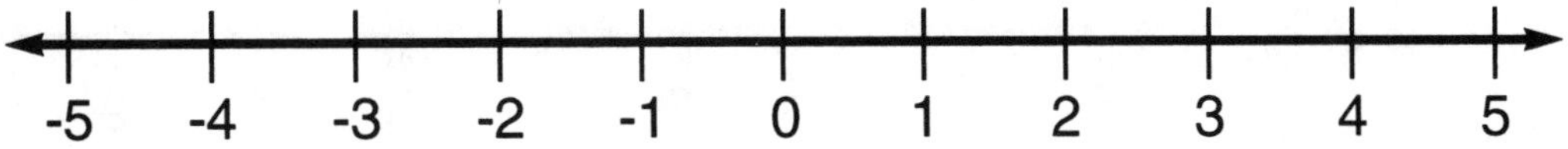

7. $d + \frac{3}{4} \geq \frac{1}{4}$

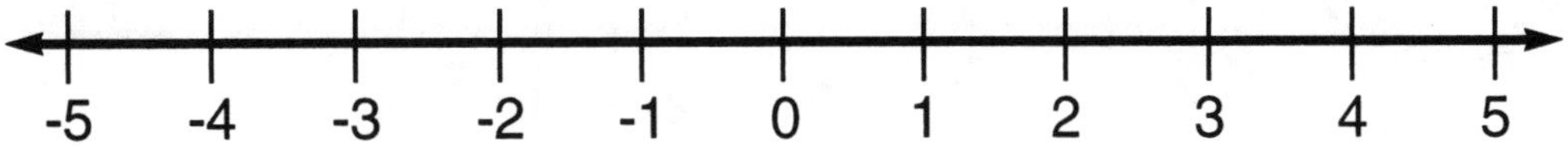

8. $7 + n \leq +8$

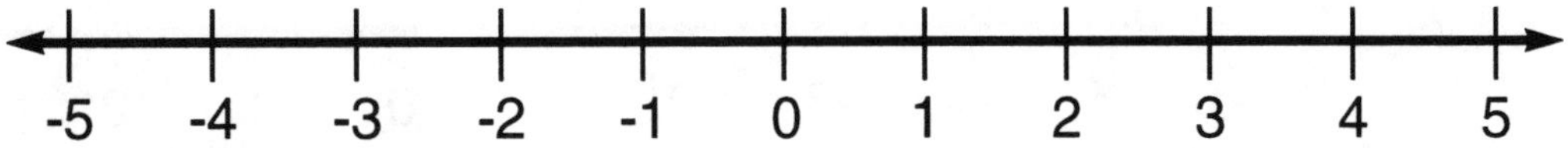

Solving Inequalities with Multiplication and Division

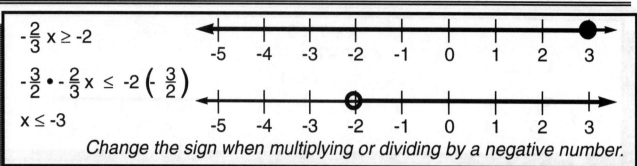

$-\frac{2}{3}x \geq -2$

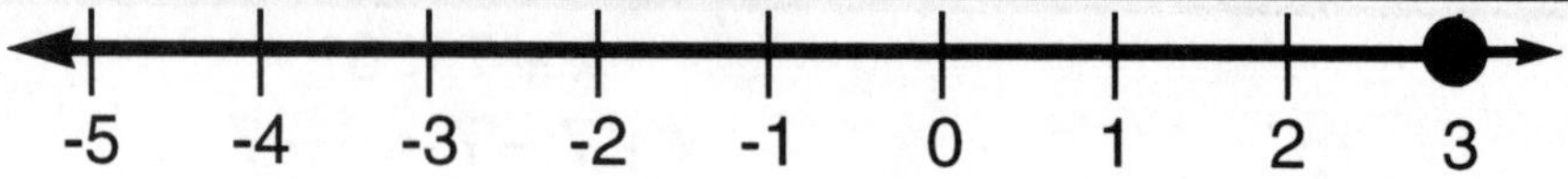

$-\frac{3}{2} \bullet -\frac{2}{3}x \leq -2\left(-\frac{3}{2}\right)$

$x \leq -3$

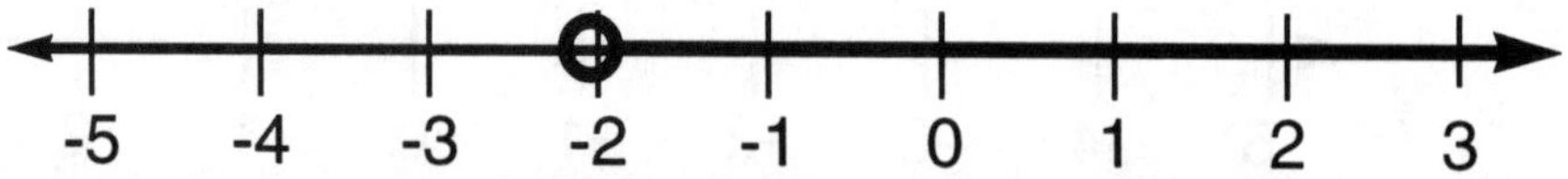

Change the sign when multiplying or dividing by a negative number.

Solve each inequality and graph on the number line.

1. $12x > 24$

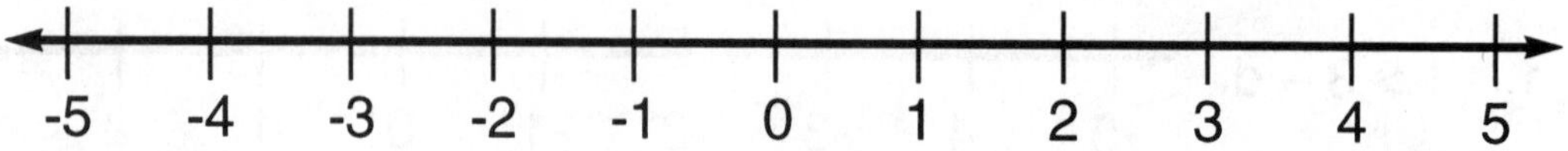

2. $-10n \leq -30$

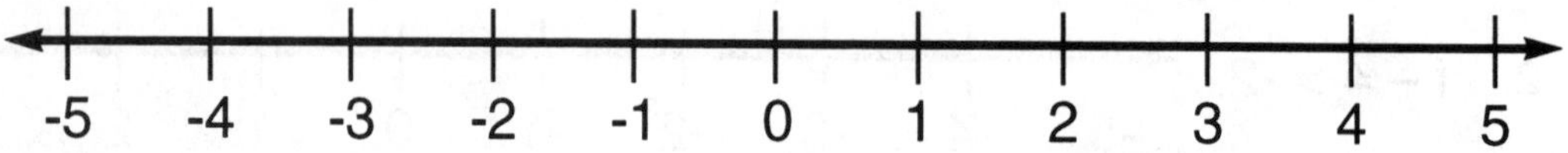

3. $1.8x \geq -5.2$

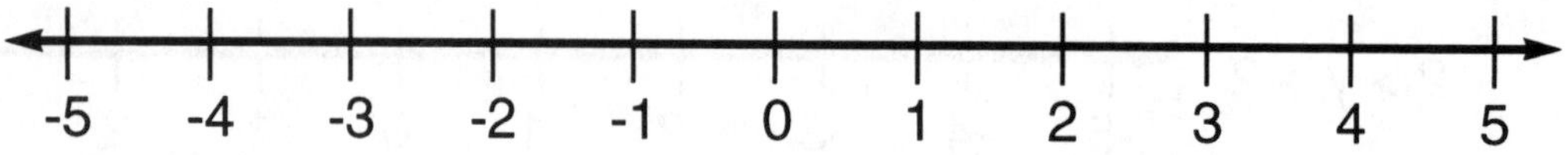

4. $-3x < 3$

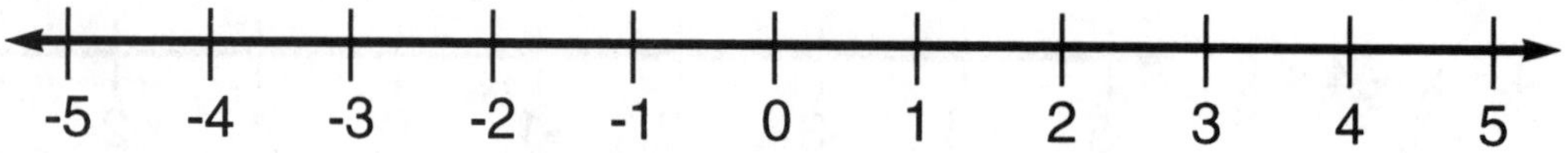

5. $n \geq -2$

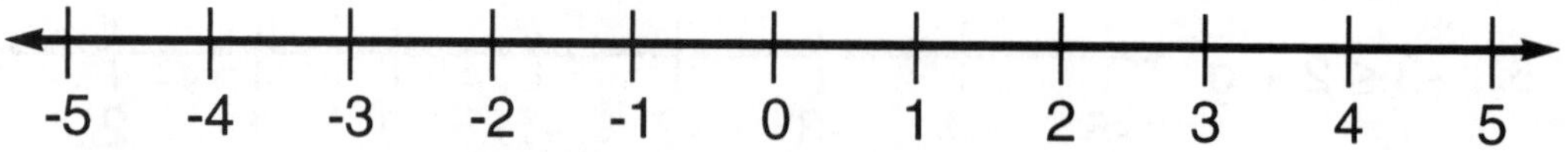

6. $-\frac{3}{4} \leq -3c$

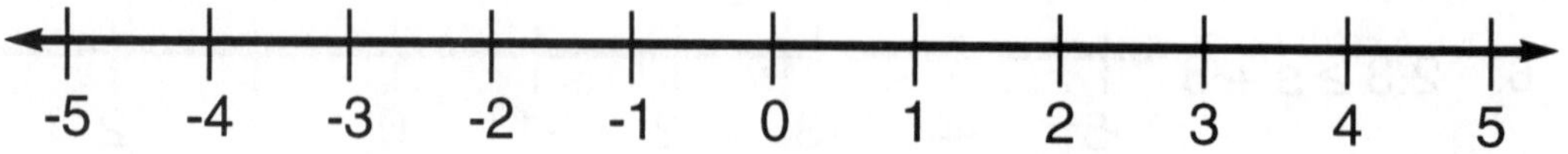

7. $2 > \frac{2}{3}z$

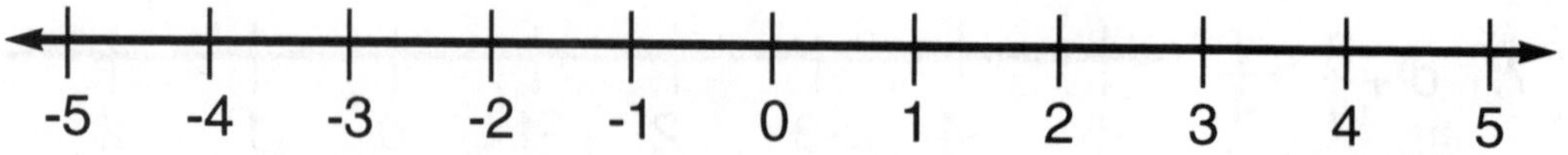

8. $2x \geq \frac{1}{2}$

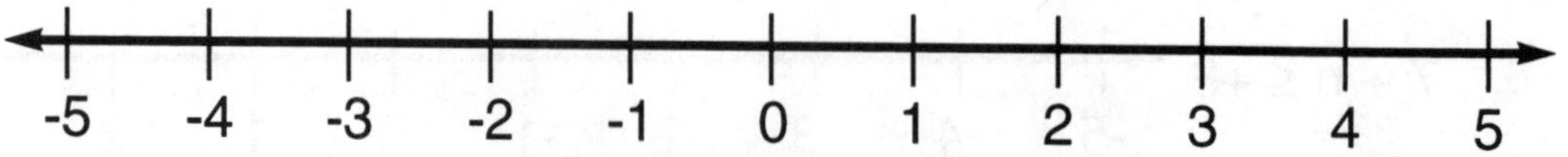

Practice Solving Inequalities

Solve each inequality and graph on the number line.

1. $3t \geq -3$

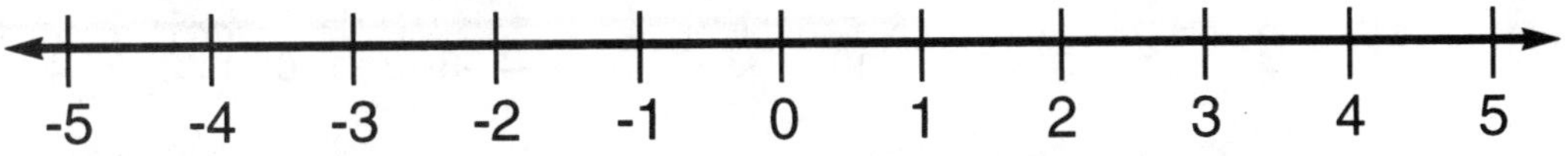

2. $-6 \geq 2b$

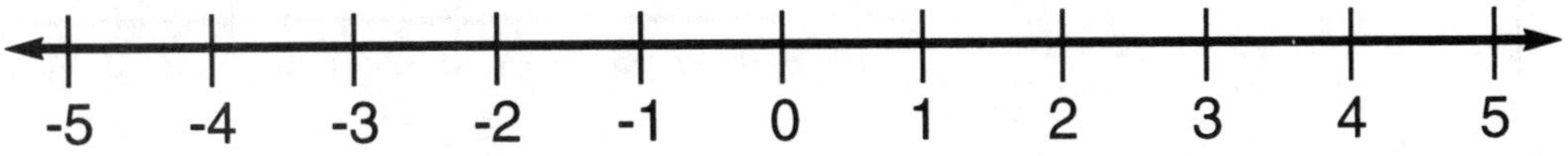

3. $2c \geq 2$

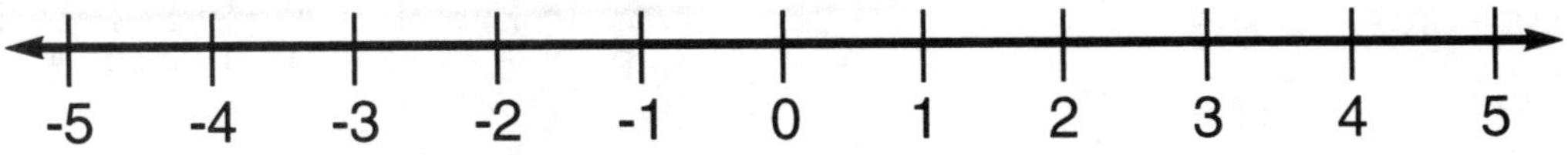

4. $e + 1 \leq 4$

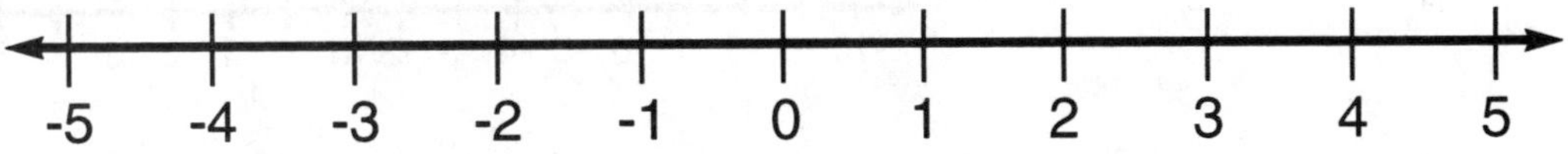

5. $m \geq -3$

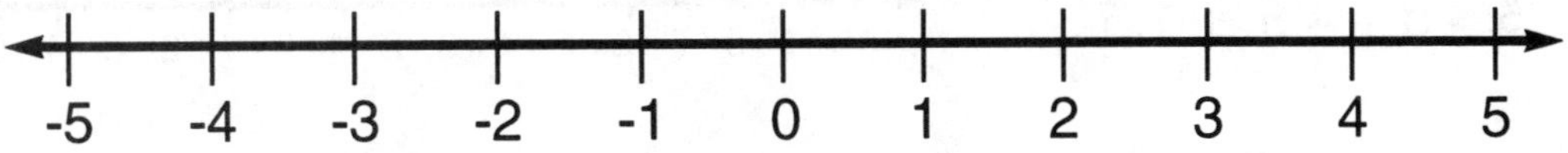

6. $x \geq 5$

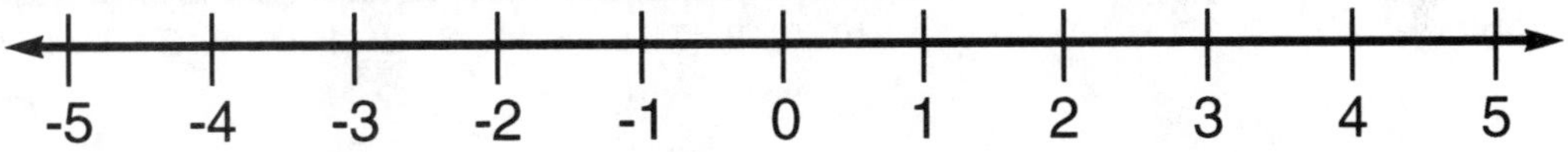

7. $-r \leq 2$

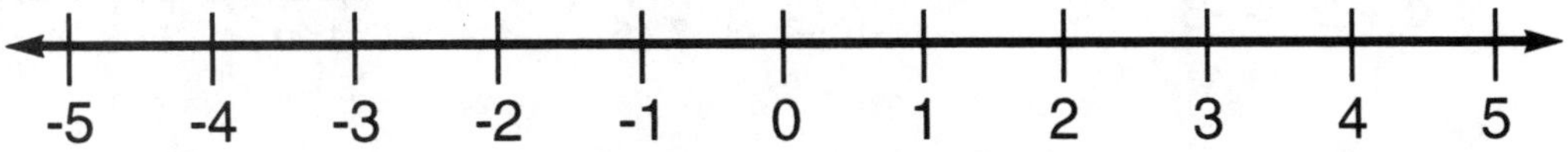

8. $t \leq -4$

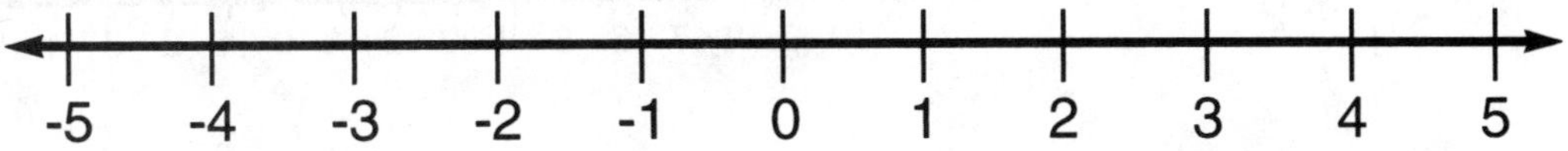

9. $x > -2$

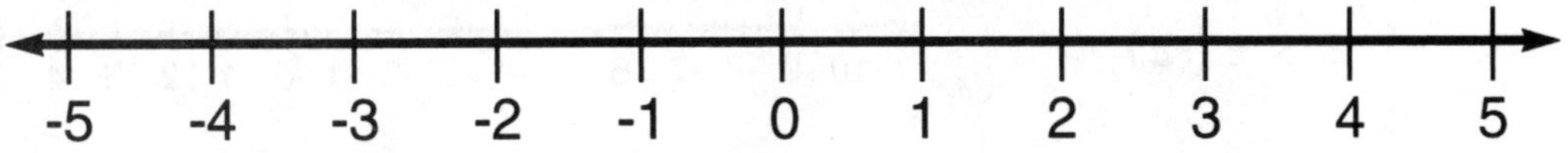

10. $r \geq 3$

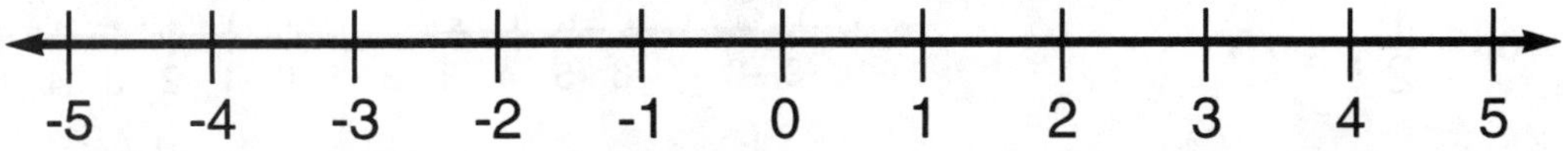

Name________________________________ *Inequalities*

Practice Solving Inequalities

Solve each inequality and graph on the number line.

1. $-13 < g - 12$

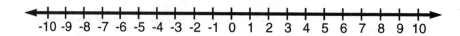

-10 -9 -8 -7 -6 -5 -4 -3 -2 -1 0 1 2 3 4 5 6 7 8 9 10

2. $-34.5 \leq x + -31.5$

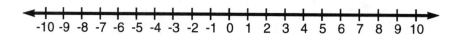

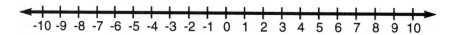

-10 -9 -8 -7 -6 -5 -4 -3 -2 -1 0 1 2 3 4 5 6 7 8 9 10

3. $8.5c < 8.5$

-10 -9 -8 -7 -6 -5 -4 -3 -2 -1 0 1 2 3 4 5 6 7 8 9 10

4. $h + 9 > 12$

-10 -9 -8 -7 -6 -5 -4 -3 -2 -1 0 1 2 3 4 5 6 7 8 9 10

5. $d + 4.5 \geq -1.5$

-10 -9 -8 -7 -6 -5 -4 -3 -2 -1 0 1 2 3 4 5 6 7 8 9 10

6. $11 > r + 14$

-10 -9 -8 -7 -6 -5 -4 -3 -2 -1 0 1 2 3 4 5 6 7 8 9 10

7. $c + 2 > -3$

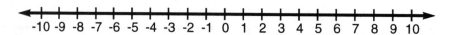

-10 -9 -8 -7 -6 -5 -4 -3 -2 -1 0 1 2 3 4 5 6 7 8 9 10

8. $-\frac{n}{3} \geq 2$

-10 -9 -8 -7 -6 -5 -4 -3 -2 -1 0 1 2 3 4 5 6 7 8 9 10

9. $-4 \geq s - (-2)$

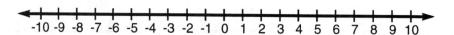

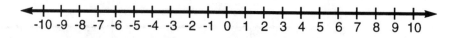

-10 -9 -8 -7 -6 -5 -4 -3 -2 -1 0 1 2 3 4 5 6 7 8 9 10

10. $\frac{1}{2}y > -5$

-10 -9 -8 -7 -6 -5 -4 -3 -2 -1 0 1 2 3 4 5 6 7 8 9 10

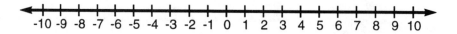

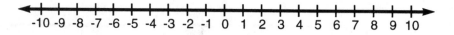

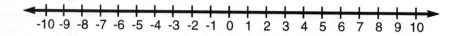

Practice Solving Inequalities

Solve each inequality and graph on the number line.

1. $-11 < k + -13$

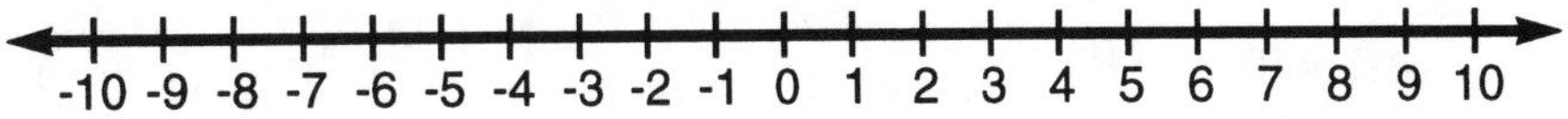

2. $-22 \geq h - 12$

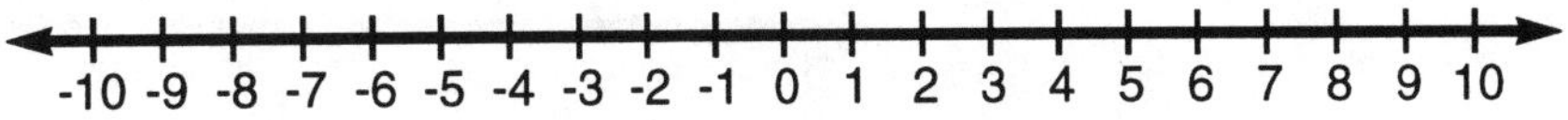

3. $3.9q \geq 11.7$

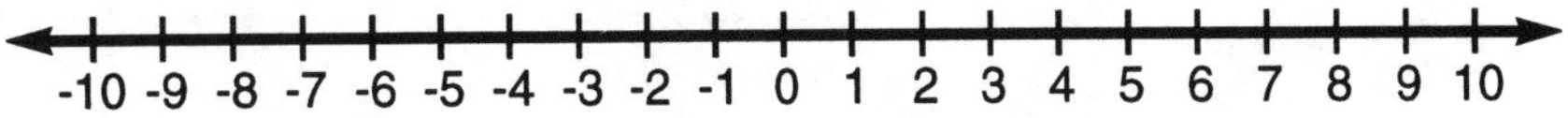

4. $13 > 12m + 7$

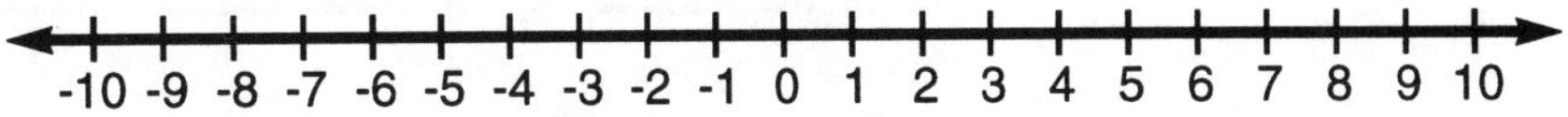

5. $a - 2.07 \geq 3.93$

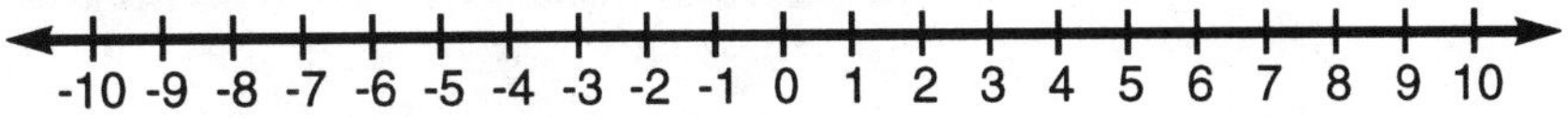

6. $-14t > 84$

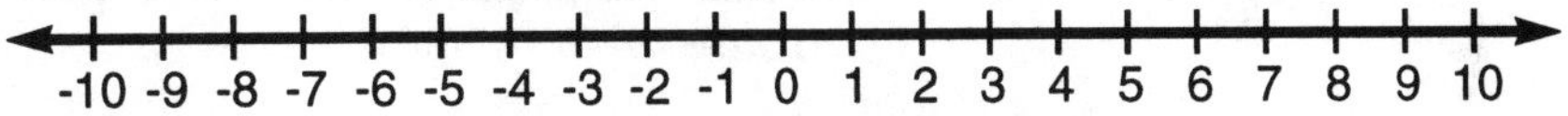

7. $h + 5 \leq -2$

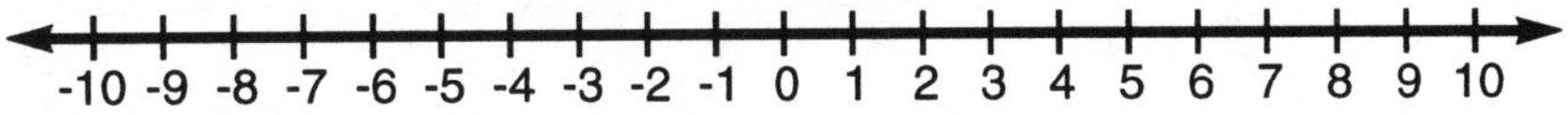

8. $-\frac{r}{2} \leq 5$

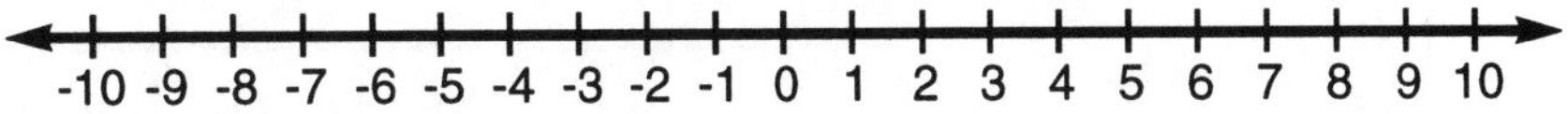

9. $-5\frac{1}{4} \geq k + \frac{3}{4}$

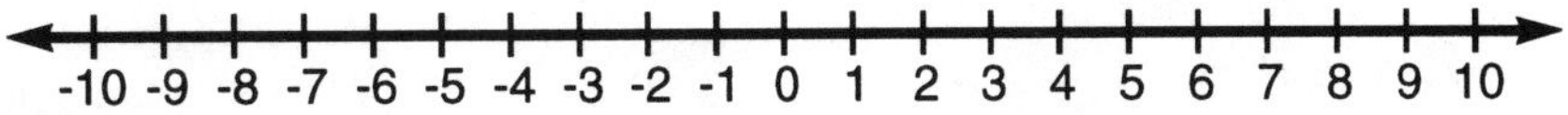

10. $\frac{2}{5}b \geq -2$

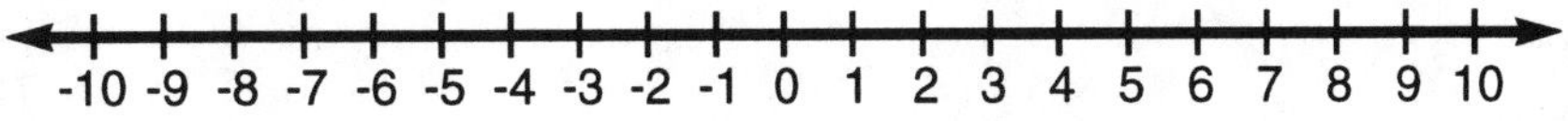

Practice Solving Inequalities

Solve each inequality and graph on the number line.

1. $-14m < m - 30$

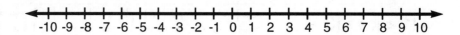

-10 -9 -8 -7 -6 -5 -4 -3 -2 -1 0 1 2 3 4 5 6 7 8 9 10

2. $-32.4 \geq j - 23.4$

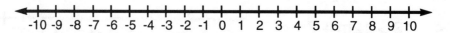

-10 -9 -8 -7 -6 -5 -4 -3 -2 -1 0 1 2 3 4 5 6 7 8 9 10

3. $2.7d \geq 21.6$

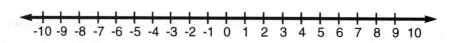

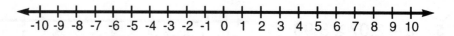

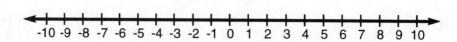

-10 -9 -8 -7 -6 -5 -4 -3 -2 -1 0 1 2 3 4 5 6 7 8 9 10

4. $7 > 9s + -2$

-10 -9 -8 -7 -6 -5 -4 -3 -2 -1 0 1 2 3 4 5 6 7 8 9 10

5. $w + 8.4 \geq 5.4$

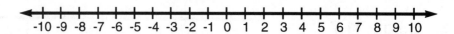

-10 -9 -8 -7 -6 -5 -4 -3 -2 -1 0 1 2 3 4 5 6 7 8 9 10

6. $-13n > 91$

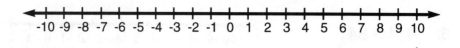

-10 -9 -8 -7 -6 -5 -4 -3 -2 -1 0 1 2 3 4 5 6 7 8 9 10

7. $k + 3\frac{2}{5} \geq -1\frac{3}{5}$

-10 -9 -8 -7 -6 -5 -4 -3 -2 -1 0 1 2 3 4 5 6 7 8 9 10

8. $-\frac{t}{3} \leq 3$

-10 -9 -8 -7 -6 -5 -4 -3 -2 -1 0 1 2 3 4 5 6 7 8 9 10

9. $-2\frac{1}{7} \leq h - \frac{1}{7}$

-10 -9 -8 -7 -6 -5 -4 -3 -2 -1 0 1 2 3 4 5 6 7 8 9 10

10. $\frac{4}{9}d \leq -4$

-10 -9 -8 -7 -6 -5 -4 -3 -2 -1 0 1 2 3 4 5 6 7 8 9 10

Solving Inequalities with Multiple Operations

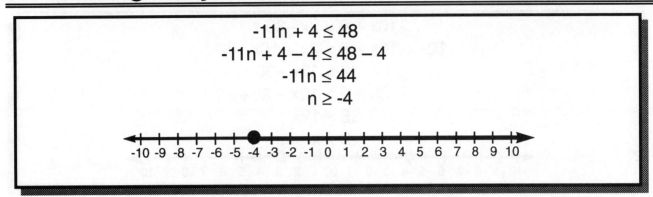

$$-11n + 4 \leq 48$$
$$-11n + 4 - 4 \leq 48 - 4$$
$$-11n \leq 44$$
$$n \geq -4$$

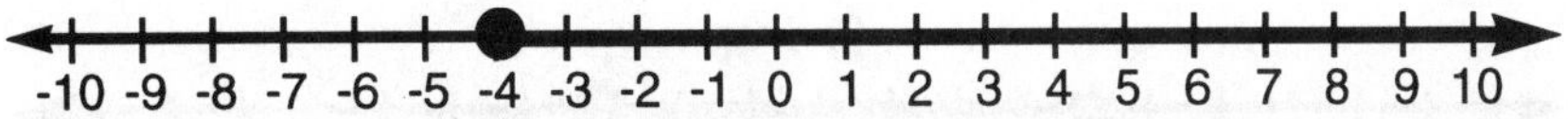

Solve each inequality and graph on the number line.

1. $6x - 3 > 21$

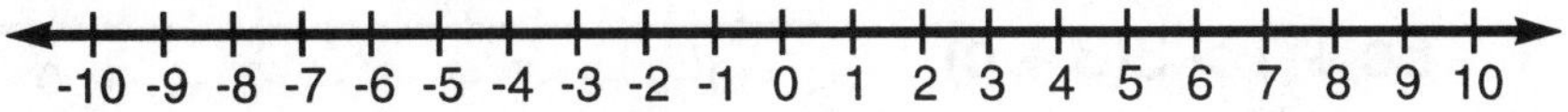

2. $5 > 4x - 7$

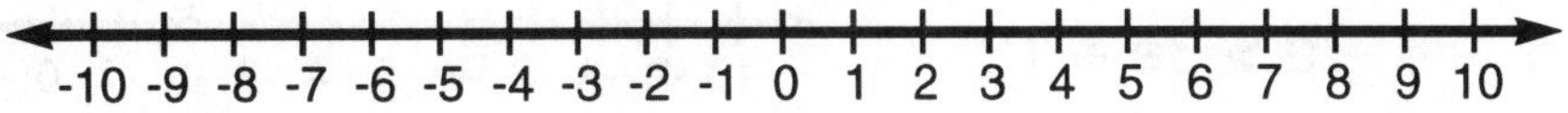

3. $3(2c - 4) \geq 48$

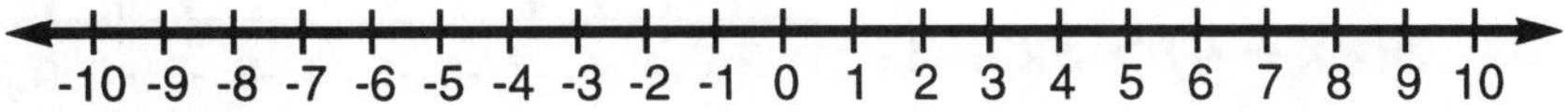

4. $-2x - 10 \geq 4$

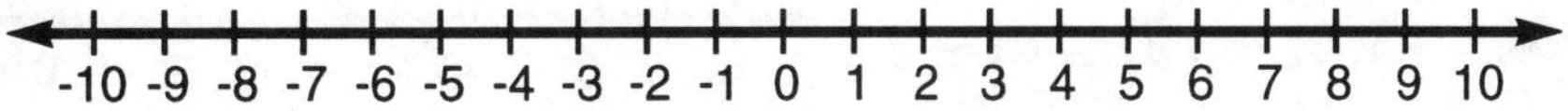

5. $-15 > -3x - 45$

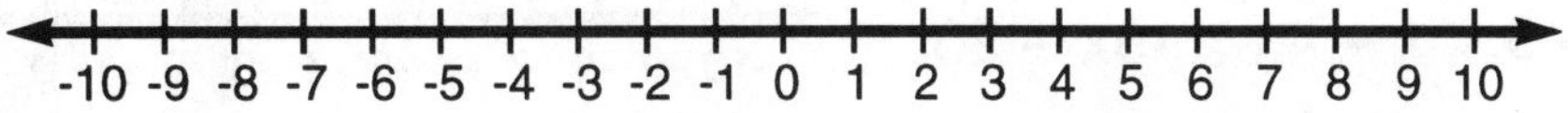

6. $-6(3t + 3) \leq 18$

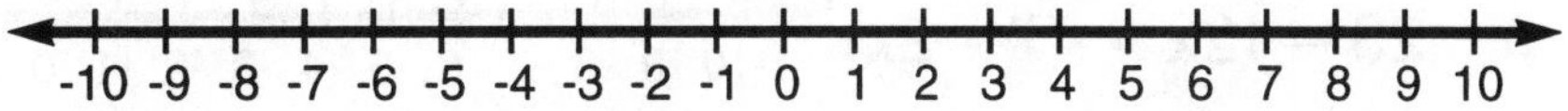

7. $-4(3x + 1) \geq 32$

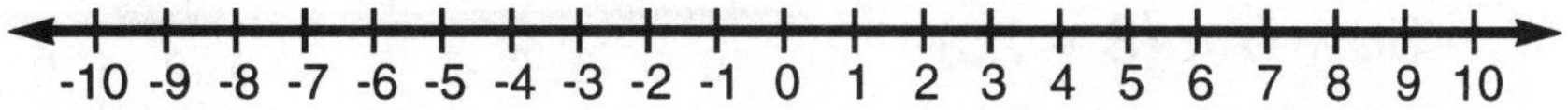

8. $31.2 < 12.8 - -2.3x$

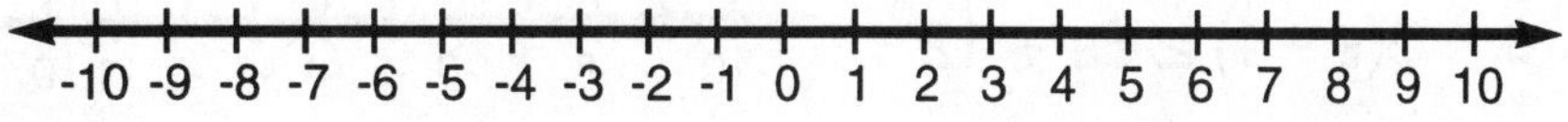

Name______________________________

Solving Inequalities with Variables on Both Sides

$$-10x + 6 > 2x - 30$$
$$-10x + 10x + 6 > 2x + 10x - 30$$
$$6 > 12x - 30$$
$$30 + 6 > 12x - 30 + 30$$
$$36 > 12x$$
$$3 > x$$

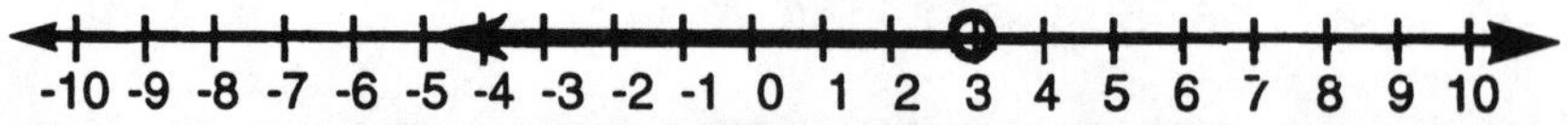

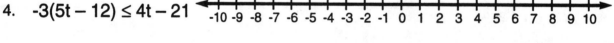

Solve each inequality and graph on the number line.

1. $5c + 1 > 3(3 + c)$

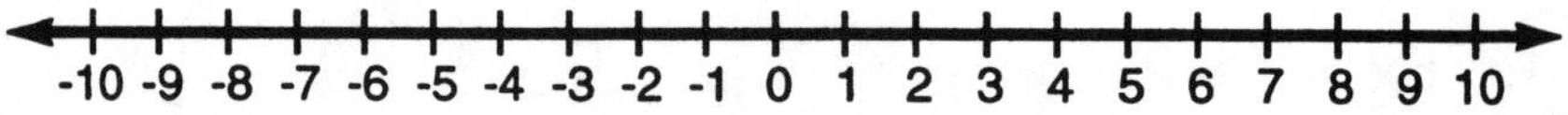

2. $8 - e > 3e + 12$

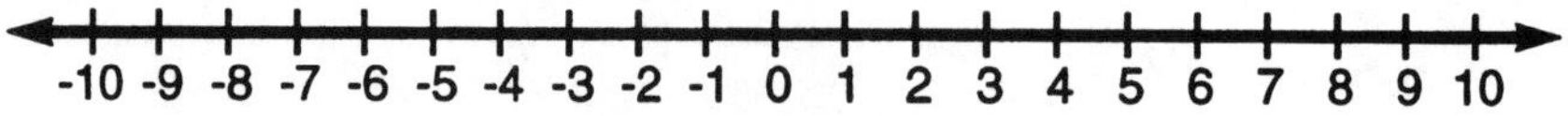

3. $3(2x - 4) > 3x + 3$

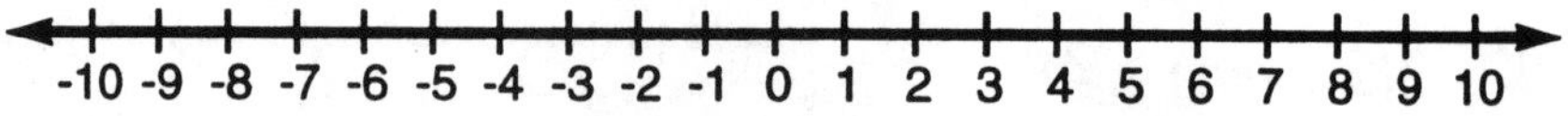

4. $-3(5t - 12) \leq 4t - 21$

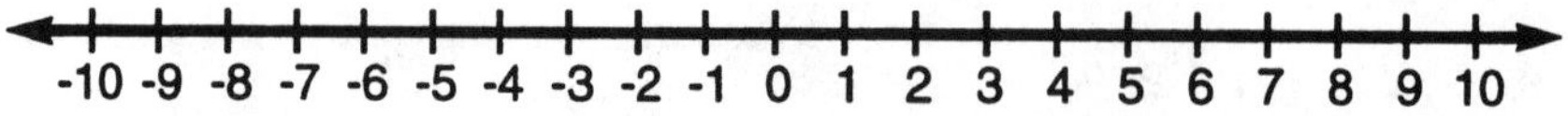

5. $x - 4x \geq -5x - 20$

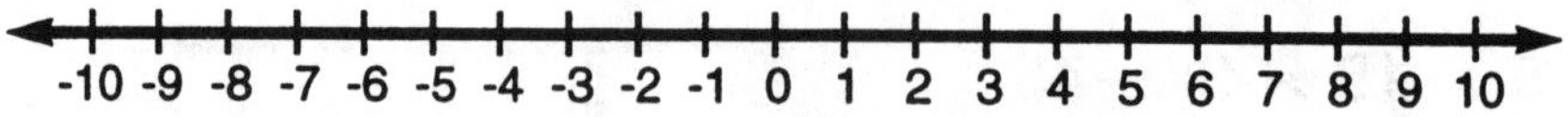

6. $23 - 12x > -(7 + 2x)$

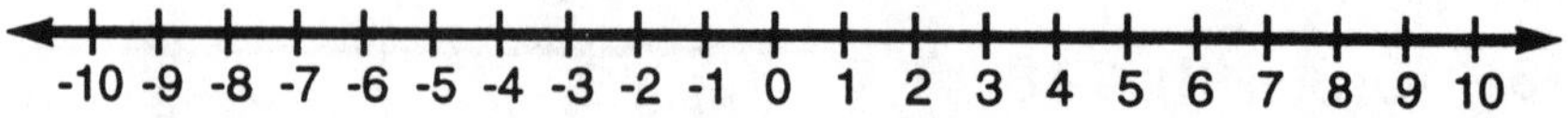

7. $5c + 6 < (3 + 2c)$

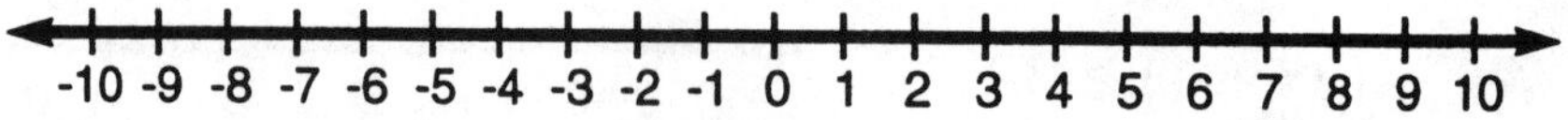

8. $3(s - 4) \geq 6s + 12$

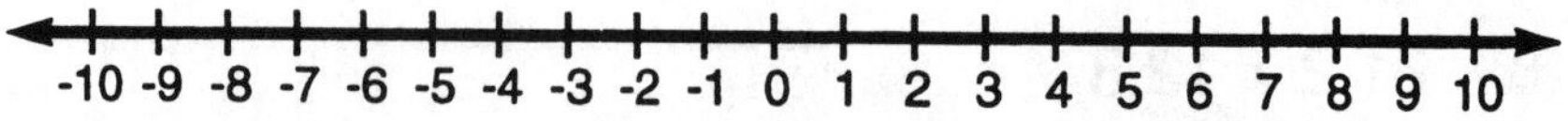

Name__________________________________

Practice Solving Inequalities

Solve each inequality and graph on the number line.

1. $12d < d + 11$

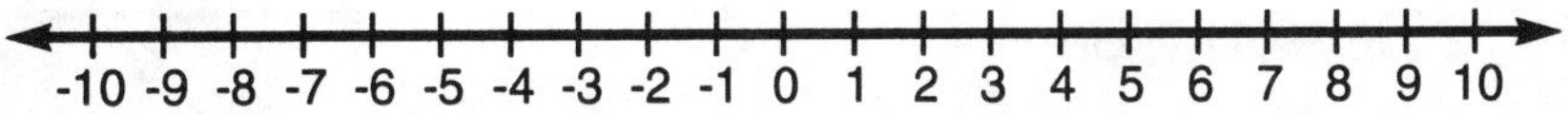

2. $32.7 \geq t + 25.7$

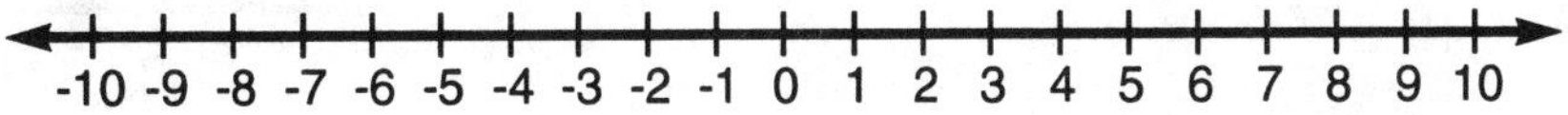

3. $2.8h \leq 12.6$

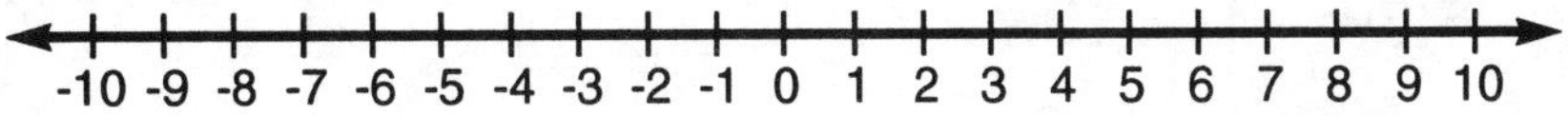

4. $9 \leq 6y - 15$

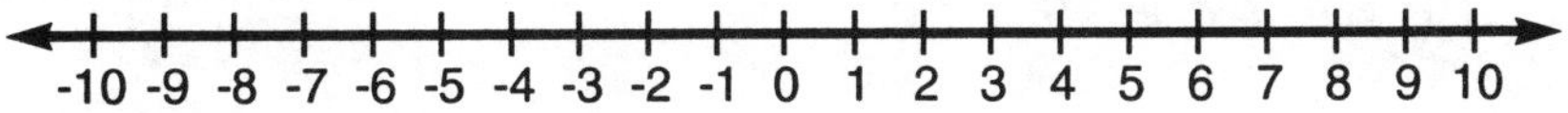

5. $2 \geq 2x - 8$

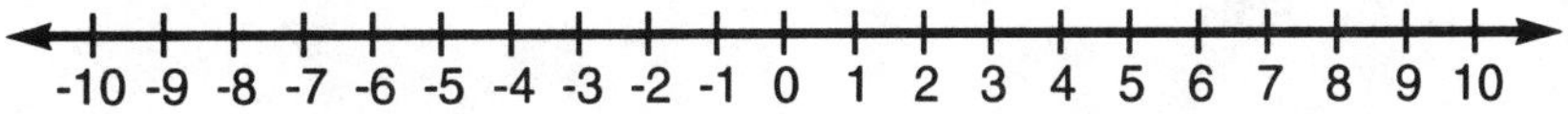

6. $-13t > 78$

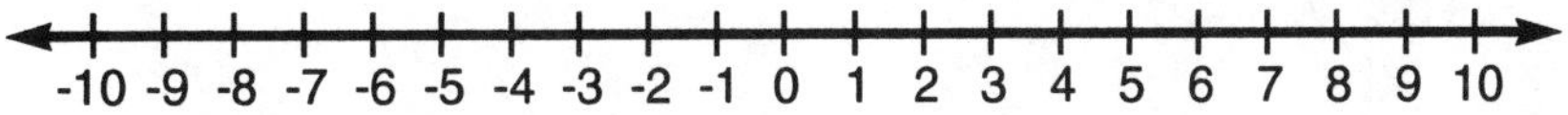

7. $r + 6 \leq 5$

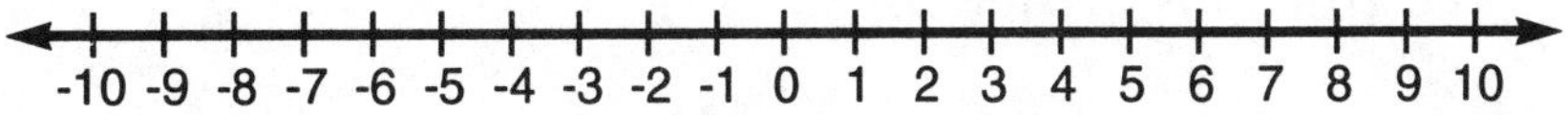

8. $-7e \geq 14$

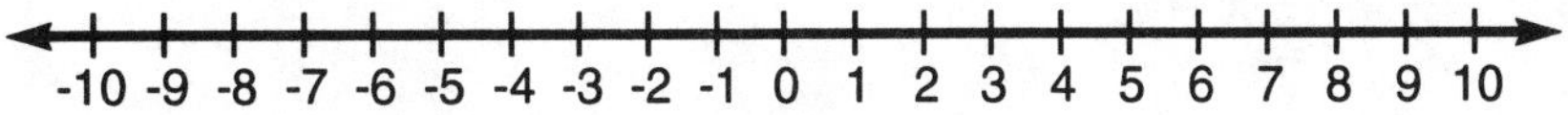

9. $-7 \geq h + 1$

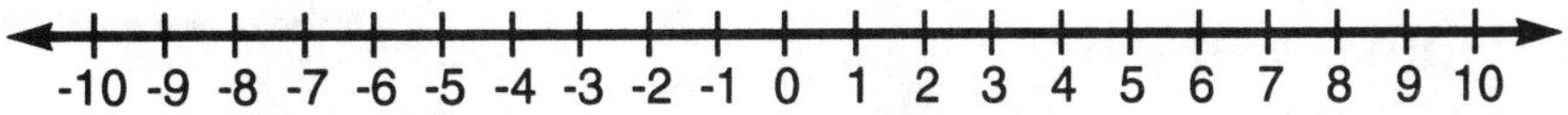

10. $\frac{2}{3}k \geq -6$

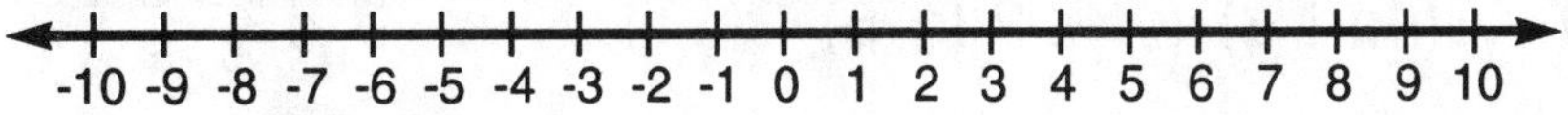

Name________________________________ *Inequalities*

Practice Solving Inequalities

Solve each inequality and graph on the number line.

1. $2(3a + 4) \geq 3a - 4$

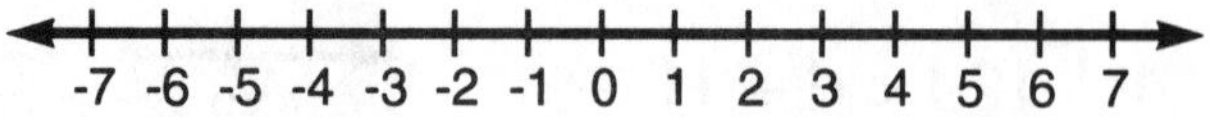

2. $4x + 7 < x - 8$

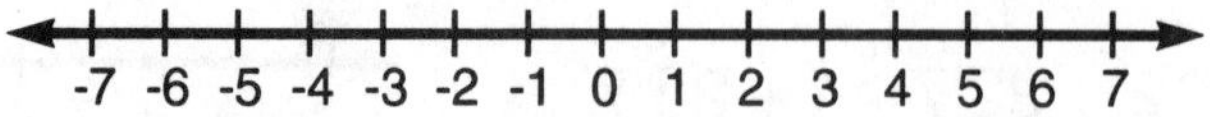

3. $5(3w - 4) < 12w + 7$

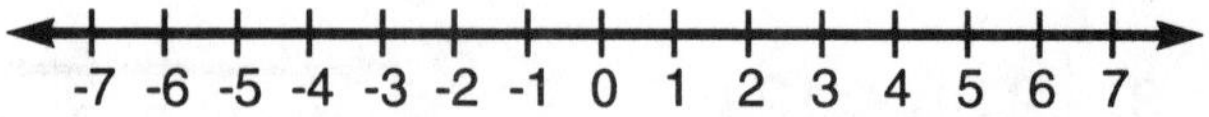

4. $8c - 7 + c < 13 + 5c$

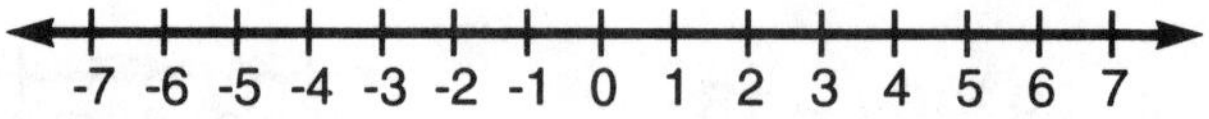

5. $13x \geq -39$

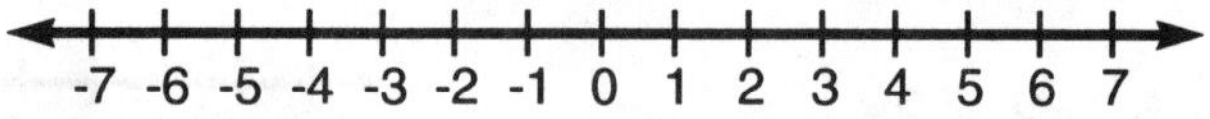

6. $48 > x + 56$

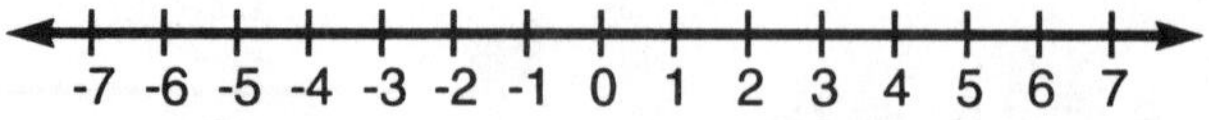

7. $12(m-1) \leq 5(m + 3) - 6$

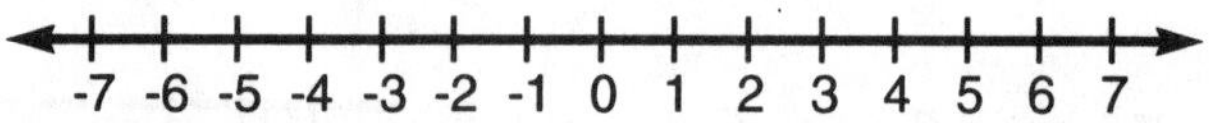

8. $\frac{1}{2} < \frac{1}{2}x - 2$

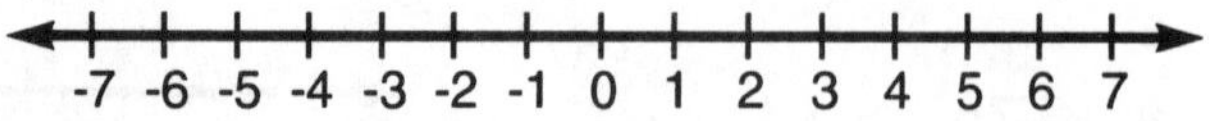

9. $-5(4a + 4) \geq 40$

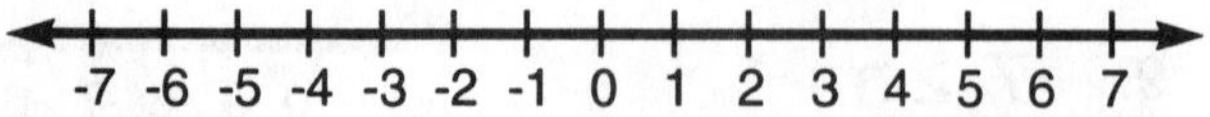

10. $3(4c + 3) + 1 \leq 2(c-5)$

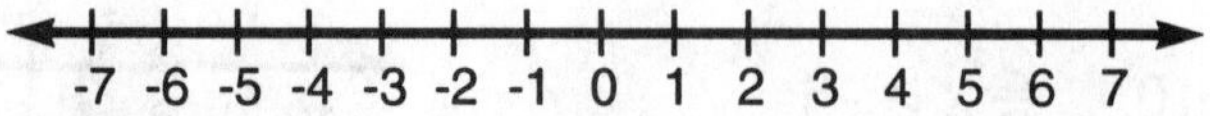

Congratulations!

____

Receives this award for

____

Keep up the great work!

________________ Signed

________________ Date

Pre-Algebra Award

____

receives this award for

____

Keep up the great work!

______________________ ______________

signed date

Algebra Whiz!

____

receives this award for

____

Great Job!

______________________ ______________

signed date

Great Work!

____

receives this award for

____

Keep up the great work!

________________________ ____________

signed date

Pre-Algebra Superstar

____

is an Algebra Superstar!

____

You are terrific!

________________________ ____________

signed date

Answer Key

Name________________________ *Fractions*

Simplifying Fractions

$\frac{3}{6} \div \frac{3}{3}$ (greatest common factor) $= \frac{1}{2}$

1. $\frac{6}{9} = \frac{2}{3}$
2. $\frac{19}{57} = \frac{1}{3}$
3. $\frac{10}{70} = \frac{1}{7}$
4. $\frac{13}{39} = \frac{1}{3}$
5. $\frac{8}{24} = \frac{1}{3}$
6. $\frac{6}{21} = \frac{2}{7}$
7. $\frac{6}{39} = \frac{2}{13}$
8. $\frac{6}{15} = \frac{2}{5}$
9. $\frac{57}{63} = \frac{19}{21}$
10. $\frac{32}{136} = \frac{4}{17}$
11. $\frac{9}{36} = \frac{1}{4}$
12. $\frac{45}{72} = \frac{5}{8}$
13. $\frac{35}{55} = \frac{7}{11}$
14. $\frac{4}{36} = \frac{1}{9}$
15. $\frac{30}{45} = \frac{2}{3}$
16. $\frac{21}{36} = \frac{7}{12}$
17. $\frac{56}{74} = \frac{28}{37}$
18. $\frac{12}{18} = \frac{2}{3}$
19. $\frac{56}{63} = \frac{8}{9}$
20. $\frac{7}{49} = \frac{1}{7}$
21. $\frac{16}{72} = \frac{2}{9}$

Name________________________ *Fractions*

Simplifying Fractions

$\frac{14}{12} \div \frac{2}{2} = \frac{7}{6}$

Improper Fraction

$\frac{14}{12} \div \frac{2}{2} = \frac{7}{6} = \frac{6}{6} + \frac{1}{6} = 1 + \frac{1}{6} = 1\frac{1}{6}$

Mixed Numeral

Write each answer as an improper fraction, then write each as a mixed numeral.

1. $\frac{63}{18} = \frac{7}{2} = 3\frac{1}{2}$
2. $\frac{45}{27} = \frac{5}{3} = 1\frac{2}{3}$
3. $\frac{28}{20} = \frac{7}{5} = 1\frac{2}{5}$
4. $\frac{15}{9} = \frac{5}{3} = 1\frac{2}{3}$
5. $\frac{36}{24} = \frac{3}{2} = 1\frac{1}{2}$
6. $\frac{27}{21} = \frac{9}{7} = 1\frac{2}{7}$
7. $\frac{30}{12} = \frac{5}{2} = 2\frac{1}{2}$
8. $\frac{69}{18} = \frac{23}{6} = 3\frac{5}{6}$
9. $\frac{50}{30} = \frac{5}{3} = 1\frac{2}{3}$
10. $\frac{20}{12} = \frac{5}{3} = 1\frac{2}{3}$
11. $\frac{28}{24} = \frac{7}{6} = 1\frac{1}{6}$
12. $\frac{26}{10} = \frac{13}{5} = 2\frac{3}{5}$
13. $\frac{20}{8} = \frac{5}{2} = 2\frac{1}{2}$
14. $\frac{45}{36} = \frac{5}{4} = 1\frac{1}{4}$

Name________________________ *Fractions*

Adding and Subtracting Fractions

When the denominators are the same, add or subtract the numerators.

$\frac{1}{6} + \frac{2}{6} = \frac{3}{6} = \frac{1}{2}$ $\frac{4}{6} - \frac{1}{6} = \frac{3}{6} = \frac{1}{2}$

Add or subtract as indicated. Reduce to lowest terms.

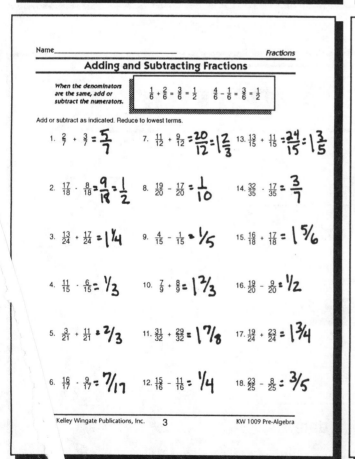

1. $\frac{2}{7} + \frac{3}{7} = \frac{5}{7}$
2. $\frac{17}{18} - \frac{8}{18} = \frac{9}{18} = \frac{1}{2}$
3. $\frac{13}{24} + \frac{17}{24} = 1\frac{1}{4}$
4. $\frac{11}{15} - \frac{6}{15} = \frac{1}{3}$
5. $\frac{3}{21} + \frac{11}{21} = \frac{2}{3}$
6. $\frac{16}{17} - \frac{9}{17} = \frac{7}{17}$
7. $\frac{11}{12} + \frac{9}{12} = \frac{20}{12} = 1\frac{2}{3}$
8. $\frac{19}{20} - \frac{17}{20} = \frac{1}{10}$
9. $\frac{4}{15} - \frac{1}{15} = \frac{1}{5}$
10. $\frac{7}{9} + \frac{8}{9} = 1\frac{2}{3}$
11. $\frac{31}{32} + \frac{29}{32} = 1\frac{7}{8}$
12. $\frac{15}{16} - \frac{11}{16} = \frac{1}{4}$
13. $\frac{13}{15} + \frac{11}{15} = \frac{24}{15} = 1\frac{3}{5}$
14. $\frac{32}{35} - \frac{17}{35} = \frac{3}{7}$
15. $\frac{16}{18} + \frac{17}{18} = 1\frac{5}{6}$
16. $\frac{19}{20} - \frac{9}{20} = \frac{1}{2}$
17. $\frac{19}{24} + \frac{23}{24} = 1\frac{3}{4}$
18. $\frac{23}{25} - \frac{8}{25} = \frac{3}{5}$

Name________________________ *Fractions*

Adding and Subtracting Fractions

When the denominators are different, find the least common multiple. In this case, 24.

$\frac{3}{8} + \frac{2}{6} = \frac{9}{24} + \frac{8}{24} = \frac{17}{24}$ $\frac{3}{8} - \frac{2}{6} = \frac{9}{24} - \frac{8}{24} = \frac{1}{24}$

Add or subtract as indicated. Reduce to lowest terms.

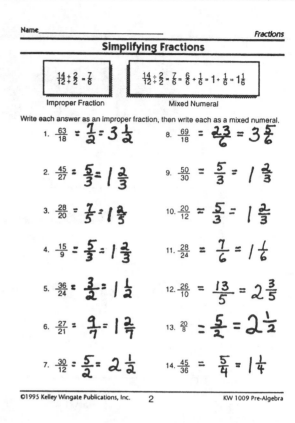

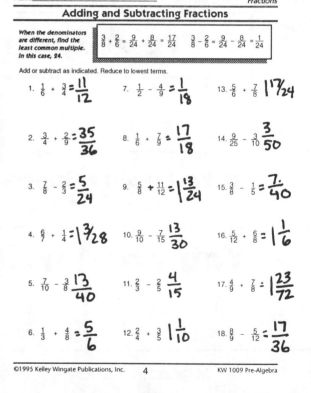

1. $\frac{1}{6} + \frac{3}{4} = \frac{11}{12}$
2. $\frac{3}{4} + \frac{2}{9} = \frac{35}{36}$
3. $\frac{7}{8} - \frac{2}{3} = \frac{5}{24}$
4. $\frac{6}{7} + \frac{1}{4} = 1\frac{3}{28}$
5. $\frac{7}{10} - \frac{3}{8}$ $\frac{13}{40}$
6. $\frac{1}{3} + \frac{4}{8} = \frac{5}{6}$
7. $\frac{1}{2} - \frac{4}{9} = \frac{1}{18}$
8. $\frac{1}{6} + \frac{7}{9} = \frac{17}{18}$
9. $\frac{5}{8} + \frac{11}{12} = 1\frac{13}{24}$
10. $\frac{9}{10} - \frac{7}{15}$ $\frac{13}{30}$
11. $\frac{2}{3} - \frac{2}{5}$ $\frac{4}{15}$
12. $\frac{2}{4} + \frac{3}{5}$ $1\frac{1}{10}$
13. $\frac{5}{6} + \frac{7}{8}$ $1\frac{17}{24}$
14. $\frac{9}{25} - \frac{3}{10}$ $\frac{3}{50}$
15. $\frac{3}{8} - \frac{1}{5} = \frac{7}{40}$
16. $\frac{5}{12} + \frac{6}{8} = 1\frac{1}{6}$
17. $\frac{4}{9} + \frac{7}{8} = 1\frac{23}{72}$
18. $\frac{8}{9} - \frac{5}{12} = \frac{17}{36}$

Answer Key

Name____________________ *Fractions*

Adding and Subtracting Fractions

When the denominators are different, find the least common multiple. In this case, 12.

$\frac{3}{4} + \frac{4}{6} = \frac{9}{12} + \frac{8}{12} = \frac{17}{12}$ $\quad \frac{3}{4} - \frac{4}{6} = \frac{9}{12} - \frac{8}{12} = \frac{1}{12}$

Add or subtract as indicated. Reduce to lowest terms.

1. $\frac{10}{12} - \frac{3}{5} = \frac{7}{30}$
2. $\frac{14}{15} + \frac{1}{6} = 1\frac{1}{10}$
3. $\frac{8}{9} + \frac{4}{5} = 1\frac{31}{45}$
4. $\frac{17}{21} - \frac{4}{6} = \frac{1}{7}$
5. $\frac{13}{15} - \frac{5}{18} = \frac{53}{90}$
6. $\frac{7}{15} + \frac{3}{6} = \frac{29}{30}$
7. $\frac{11}{12} - \frac{5}{18}$ $\frac{23}{36}$
8. $\frac{3}{10} + \frac{7}{15} = \frac{23}{30}$
9. $\frac{5}{6} - \frac{3}{8} = \frac{11}{24}$
10. $\frac{5}{8} + \frac{2}{7} = \frac{51}{56}$
11. $\frac{6}{7} - \frac{3}{5}$ $\frac{9}{35}$
12. $\frac{7}{8} + \frac{9}{10} = 1\frac{31}{40}$
13. $\frac{7}{12} + \frac{7}{8}$ $1\frac{11}{24}$
14. $\frac{2}{6} + \frac{3}{9}$ $\frac{2}{3}$
15. $\frac{4}{15} - \frac{3}{12}$ $\frac{1}{60}$
16. $\frac{29}{32} + \frac{7}{8}$ $1\frac{25}{32}$
17. $\frac{11}{14} - \frac{1}{6}$ $\frac{13}{21}$
18. $\frac{4}{5} + \frac{11}{15}$ $1\frac{8}{15}$

Name____________________ *Fractions*

Adding and Subtracting Mixed Numbers

When the denominators are different, find the least common multiple. In this case, 8.

$3\frac{1}{4} + 1\frac{3}{8} = 3\frac{2}{8} + 1\frac{3}{8} = 4\frac{5}{8}$

1. $4\frac{5}{8} - 2\frac{2}{6} = 2\frac{7}{24}$
2. $8\frac{1}{6} + 5\frac{3}{4} = 13\frac{11}{12}$
3. $3\frac{7}{12} + 7\frac{5}{6} = 11\frac{5}{12}$
4. $12 - 3\frac{1}{5} = 8\frac{4}{5}$
5. $1\frac{9}{10} - 1\frac{3}{4} = \frac{3}{20}$
6. $5\frac{1}{2} - 2\frac{2}{7} = 3\frac{3}{14}$
7. $9\frac{3}{5} + 4\frac{2}{3} = 14\frac{4}{15}$
8. $16\frac{1}{3} - 7\frac{5}{8} = 8\frac{17}{24}$
9. $4\frac{1}{8} - 3\frac{1}{2} = \frac{5}{8}$
10. $12\frac{7}{9} + 3\frac{2}{3}$ $16\frac{4}{9}$
11. $4\frac{8}{9} + 2\frac{5}{6} = 7\frac{13}{18}$
12. $3\frac{8}{12} - 1\frac{5}{18} = 2\frac{7}{18}$
13. $7\frac{1}{2} - 2\frac{7}{10} = 4\frac{4}{5}$
14. $6\frac{2}{7} - 1\frac{1}{3} = 4\frac{20}{21}$
15. $17\frac{3}{4} - 8\frac{2}{5} = 9\frac{7}{20}$
16. $6\frac{4}{5} + 2\frac{3}{8} = 9\frac{7}{40}$
17. $11\frac{4}{5} - 3\frac{5}{6} = 7\frac{29}{30}$
18. $4\frac{3}{6} + 7\frac{3}{8} = 11\frac{7}{8}$

Name____________________ *Fractions*

Practice Adding and Subtracting Fractions

When the denominators are different, find the least common multiple. In this case, 9.

$2\frac{2}{3} + 6\frac{4}{9} = 2\frac{6}{9} + 6\frac{4}{9} = 8\frac{10}{9} = 9\frac{1}{9}$

1. $5\frac{1}{2} - 3\frac{5}{6} = 1\frac{2}{3}$
2. $9 - 6\frac{1}{3} = 2\frac{2}{3}$
3. $7\frac{3}{8} + 4\frac{1}{4} = 11\frac{5}{8}$
4. $12\frac{2}{7} - 3\frac{5}{6}$ $8\frac{19}{42}$
5. $8\frac{1}{3} + 6\frac{7}{9} = 15\frac{1}{9}$
6. $15\frac{7}{8} - 4\frac{2}{9}$ $11\frac{47}{72}$
7. $7\frac{8}{12} - 5\frac{1}{3} = 2\frac{1}{3}$
8. $14\frac{3}{4} - 8\frac{5}{6} = 5\frac{11}{12}$
9. $3\frac{7}{12} + 6\frac{12}{18} = 10\frac{1}{4}$
10. $5\frac{3}{10} - 3\frac{9}{12} = 1\frac{11}{20}$
11. $10\frac{10}{12} - 3\frac{4}{6} = 7\frac{1}{6}$
12. $9\frac{15}{18} + 5\frac{4}{12} = 15\frac{1}{6}$
13. $5\frac{5}{9} + 3\frac{4}{6} = 9\frac{2}{9}$
14. $8\frac{2}{9} + 3\frac{3}{6} = 11\frac{13}{18}$
15. $6\frac{2}{7} - 5\frac{3}{14} = 1\frac{1}{14}$
16. $9\frac{8}{11} + 4\frac{1}{2} = 14\frac{5}{22}$
17. $13\frac{4}{21} - 8\frac{2}{3} = 4\frac{11}{21}$
18. $7\frac{7}{12} - 3\frac{4}{7} = 4\frac{1}{84}$

Name____________________ *Fractions*

Multiplying Fractions

$1\frac{2}{3} \cdot 2\frac{1}{2} = \frac{5}{3} \cdot \frac{5}{2} = \frac{25}{6}$ or $4\frac{1}{6}$ (rewrite, rewrite)

1. $\frac{3}{5} \cdot \frac{15}{18} = \frac{1}{2}$
2. $\frac{2}{3} \cdot \frac{21}{24} = \frac{7}{12}$
3. $5\frac{1}{2} \cdot \frac{2}{11} = 1$
4. $7\frac{2}{7} \cdot 2\frac{1}{3} = 17$
5. $5\frac{3}{5} \cdot 2\frac{1}{7} = 12$
6. $3\frac{12}{13} \cdot 4\frac{1}{3} = 17$
7. $4\frac{4}{7} \cdot 1\frac{3}{4} = 8$
8. $8\frac{1}{3} \cdot 6\frac{3}{5} = 55$
9. $3\frac{1}{5} \cdot 12\frac{1}{2} = 40$
10. $1\frac{1}{2} \cdot 3\frac{1}{5} = 4\frac{4}{5}$
11. $9\frac{1}{3} \cdot 2\frac{1}{7} = 20$
12. $2\frac{3}{4} \cdot 1\frac{1}{3} = 3\frac{2}{3}$
13. $4\frac{5}{6} \cdot 5\frac{1}{7} = 24\frac{6}{7}$
14. $12\frac{2}{3} \cdot 7\frac{1}{2}$ 95
15. $5\frac{2}{3} \cdot 8\frac{1}{4}$ $46\frac{3}{4}$
16. $10\frac{2}{3} \cdot 7\frac{1}{8} = 76$
17. $2\frac{4}{7} \cdot 2\frac{3}{9} = 6$
18. $5\frac{3}{12} \cdot 2\frac{1}{7} = 11\frac{1}{4}$

Answer Key

Name____________________ *Fractions*

Multiplying Fractions

$\underbrace{2\frac{1}{3}}_{\text{rewrite}} \cdot \underbrace{1\frac{1}{2}}_{\text{rewrite}} = \frac{7}{3} \cdot \frac{3}{2} = \frac{21}{6}$ or $3\frac{3}{6}$ or $3\frac{1}{2}$

1. $12\frac{1}{2} \cdot 8\frac{2}{5} = 105$
2. $8\frac{3}{4} \cdot 1\frac{3}{7} = 12\frac{1}{2}$
3. $13\frac{1}{3} \cdot 2\frac{2}{5} = 32$
4. $5\frac{5}{7} \cdot 9\frac{4}{5} = 56$
5. $7\frac{1}{8} \cdot 9\frac{1}{3} = 66\frac{1}{2}$
6. $4\frac{2}{3} \cdot 7\frac{1}{2} = 35$
7. $3\frac{1}{3} \cdot 9\frac{3}{4} = 32\frac{1}{2}$
8. $7\frac{1}{3} \cdot 4\frac{1}{2} = 33$
9. $6\frac{2}{9} \cdot 3\frac{6}{8} = 23\frac{1}{3}$
10. $3\frac{3}{5} \cdot 2\frac{7}{9} = 10$
11. $3\frac{8}{9} \cdot 5\frac{2}{5} = 21$
12. $4\frac{7}{12} \cdot 6\frac{2}{5} = 29\frac{1}{3}$
13. $8\frac{2}{5} \cdot 3\frac{4}{7} = 30$
14. $15\frac{3}{4} \cdot 6\frac{2}{7} = 99$
15. $8\frac{4}{5} \cdot 2\frac{5}{10} = 22$
16. $10\frac{1}{2} \cdot 7\frac{1}{3} = 77$
17. $5\frac{4}{9} \cdot 2\frac{4}{7} = 14$
18. $11\frac{2}{3} \cdot 4\frac{4}{5} = 56$

©1995 Kelley Wingate Publications, Inc. 9 KW 1009 Pre-Algebra

Name____________________ *Fractions*

Dividing Fractions

$\underbrace{1\frac{2}{3} \div 2\frac{1}{2}}_{\text{rewrite}} = \frac{5}{3} \div \frac{5}{2} = \frac{5}{3} \cdot \frac{2}{5} = \frac{2}{3}$ (invert and multiply)

1. $6\frac{2}{3} \div 3\frac{4}{12} = 2$
2. $4\frac{1}{2} \div 5\frac{1}{4} = \frac{6}{7}$
3. $2\frac{2}{9} \div 4\frac{1}{6} = \frac{8}{15}$
4. $6\frac{2}{3} \div 4\frac{4}{9} = 1\frac{1}{2}$
5. $8\frac{3}{4} \div 2\frac{1}{2} = 3\frac{1}{2}$
6. $7\frac{3}{5} \div 1\frac{9}{10} = 4$
7. $3\frac{1}{3} \div 1\frac{5}{9} = 2\frac{1}{7}$
8. $4\frac{3}{8} \div 2\frac{1}{12} = 2\frac{1}{10}$
9. $9\frac{2}{7} \div 2\frac{2}{14} = 4\frac{1}{3}$
10. $7\frac{1}{5} \div 3\frac{3}{5} = 2$
11. $7\frac{3}{4} \div 1\frac{1}{4} = 6\frac{1}{5}$
12. $5\frac{2}{5} \div 4\frac{1}{2} = 1\frac{1}{5}$
13. $2\frac{7}{10} \div 3\frac{9}{15} = \frac{3}{4}$
14. $2\frac{2}{6} \div 4\frac{2}{3} = \frac{1}{2}$
15. $3\frac{1}{2} \div 4\frac{1}{3} = \frac{21}{26}$
16. $3\frac{3}{4} \div 1\frac{2}{3} = 2\frac{1}{4}$
17. $9\frac{4}{5} \div 1\frac{4}{10} = 7$
18. $3\frac{1}{5} \div 1\frac{6}{10} = 2$

©1995 Kelley Wingate Publications, Inc. 10 KW 1009 Pre-Algebra

Name____________________ *Fractions*

Dividing Fractions

$\underbrace{1\frac{2}{3} \div 2\frac{1}{2}}_{\text{rewrite}} = \frac{5}{3} \div \frac{5}{2} = \frac{5}{3} \cdot \frac{2}{5} = \frac{2}{3}$ (invert and multiply)

1. $7\frac{4}{5} \div 1\frac{3}{10} = 6$
2. $5\frac{1}{2} \div 8\frac{4}{5} = \frac{5}{8}$
3. $9\frac{2}{7} \div 3\frac{3}{14} = 2\frac{8}{9}$
4. $8\frac{2}{3} \div 2\frac{1}{10} = 4$
5. $3\frac{5}{7} \div 3\frac{15}{21} = 1$
6. $8\frac{2}{7} \div 2\frac{1}{14} = 4$
7. $9\frac{1}{6} \div 3\frac{8}{12} = 2\frac{1}{2}$
8. $11\frac{3}{7} \div 5\frac{10}{14} = 2$
9. $7\frac{1}{9} \div 2\frac{2}{3} = 2\frac{2}{3}$
10. $9\frac{3}{5} \div 1\frac{6}{10} = 6$
11. $12\frac{3}{5} \div 2\frac{7}{10} = 4\frac{2}{3}$
12. $8\frac{1}{3} \div 4\frac{1}{6} = 2$
13. $7\frac{1}{2} \div 8\frac{3}{4} = \frac{6}{7}$
14. $9\frac{1}{5} \div 2\frac{3}{10} = 4$
15. $12\frac{4}{5} \div 1\frac{1}{15} = 12$
16. $10\frac{4}{5} \div 1\frac{8}{10} = 6$
17. $13\frac{3}{4} \div 5\frac{1}{2} = 2\frac{1}{2}$
18. $3\frac{3}{4} \div 3\frac{1}{8} = 1\frac{1}{5}$

©1995 Kelley Wingate Publications, Inc. 11 KW 1009 Pre-Algebra

Name____________________ *Fractions*

Fractions Practice

Perform the indicated operation for each pair of fractions below.

1. $5\frac{3}{5} + 8\frac{1}{4} = 13\frac{17}{20}$
2. $15\frac{3}{4} \cdot 3\frac{3}{7} = 54$
3. $12\frac{1}{9} - 7\frac{5}{6} = 4\frac{5}{18}$
4. $7\frac{1}{2} \div 4\frac{1}{6} = 1\frac{4}{5}$
5. $\frac{7}{9} \cdot \frac{3}{14} = \frac{1}{6}$
6. $5\frac{5}{8} \cdot 5\frac{1}{3} = 30$
7. $4\frac{2}{5} \div 3\frac{3}{10} = 1\frac{1}{3}$
8. $7\frac{1}{2} + 9\frac{3}{5} = 17\frac{1}{10}$
9. $\frac{3}{5} \div \frac{4}{5} = \frac{3}{4}$
10. $11\frac{1}{2} - 2\frac{3}{7} = 9\frac{1}{14}$
11. $15\frac{5}{6} + 3\frac{4}{9} = 19\frac{5}{18}$
12. $9\frac{3}{5} \div 3\frac{6}{10} = 2\frac{2}{3}$
13. $8 - 3\frac{2}{7} = 4\frac{5}{7}$
14. $5\frac{7}{12} - 3\frac{15}{36} = 36$
15. $7\frac{3}{5} + 4\frac{7}{8} = 12\frac{19}{40}$
16. $9\frac{1}{3} \div 2\frac{4}{12} = 4$
17. $4\frac{4}{5} \cdot 3\frac{3}{4} = 18$
18. $4\frac{2}{15} - 1\frac{11}{12} = 2\frac{13}{60}$
19. $4\frac{6}{3} + 6\frac{2}{3} = 12\frac{2}{3}$
20. $6\frac{6}{45} - 2\frac{4}{45} = 4\frac{2}{45}$
21. $8\frac{6}{30} + 6\frac{5}{15} = 14\frac{8}{15}$

©1995 Kelley Wingate Publications, Inc. 12 KW 1009 Pre-Algebra

Answer Key

Name________________________ *Fractions*

Problem Solving With Fractions

A recipe calls for $\frac{3}{4}$ pound of rasins and $\frac{1}{2}$ pound of dates. How many pounds are needed in all? $\frac{3}{4} + \frac{1}{2} = 1\frac{1}{4}$

1. A football team played 27 games and won $\frac{2}{3}$ of them.
   How many games did the team win? 18
   How many games did the team lose? 9

2. A punch recipe calls for $\frac{2}{3}$ cup of apple juice, $\frac{3}{4}$ cup of orange juice, 1 cup of lemon juice, and $\frac{1}{2}$ cup of lime juice. How many cups of juice are needed to make this punch? $2\frac{11}{12}$

3. Evie went to the grocery store to buy some ceral. A one-pound box of cereal costs $2.25. A one-half pound box of cereal costs $1.65. How much money would Evie save if she bought a 1 pound box of cereal instead of 2 one-half boxes? $1.05

4. Delaney wants to make a wedding cake. The recipe calls for $8\frac{1}{2}$ cups of flour. A 16-ounce bag contains 2 cups. How many bags of flour must Delaney buy in order to make her cake? 5

5. If $2\frac{1}{2}$ pounds of apples cost $2.35 and $2\frac{2}{3}$ pounds of strawberries cost $2.50, which fruit is less expensive per pound? SAME

6. A cookie recipe calls for $1\frac{1}{3}$ cups of flour, $1\frac{2}{3}$ cups of sugar, $2\frac{2}{3}$ cups of rasins, and $3\frac{2}{3}$ cups of walnuts. How many cups of dry ingredients are needed for this recipe? $9\frac{1}{3}$

 13 KW 1009 Pre-Algebra

Name________________________ *Fractions*

Changing Fractions to Decimals

$\frac{1}{4} \rightarrow 4\overline{)1.00}$ = .25 (4 into 1.00: 80, 20, 20, 0) $\rightarrow \frac{1}{4} = .25$ terminating

$\frac{1}{3} \rightarrow 3\overline{)1.00}$ = .3333 (3 into 1.00: 9, 10, 9, 10, 9, 10) $\rightarrow \frac{1}{3} = .\overline{333}$ repeating

Change to fractions.

1. $\frac{3}{4} = 0.75$
2. $\frac{6}{16} = 0.375$
3. $\frac{18}{22} = 0.\overline{81}$
4. $\frac{5}{16} = 0.3125$
5. $\frac{7}{15} = 0.4\overline{6}$
6. $\frac{2}{3} = 0.\overline{6}$
7. $\frac{25}{37} = 0.\overline{675}$
8. $\frac{11}{13} = 0.\overline{846153}$
9. $\frac{23}{33} = 0.\overline{69}$
10. $3\frac{1}{4} = 3.25$
11. $\frac{4}{33} = 0.\overline{12}$
12. $\frac{13}{15} = 0.8\overline{6}$
13. $\frac{12}{25} = 0.48$
14. $\frac{1}{9} = 0.\overline{1}$
15. $1\frac{3}{5} = 1.6$

 14 KW 1009 Pre-Algebra

Name________________________ *Fractions*

Changing Fractions to Decimals

1. $\frac{6}{9} = 0.\overline{6}$
2. $\frac{19}{57} = 0.\overline{3}$
3. $\frac{10}{70} = 0.\overline{142857}$
4. $\frac{13}{39}$ $0.\overline{3}$
5. $\frac{8}{24} = 0.\overline{3}$
6. $\frac{6}{21} = 0.\overline{285714}$
7. $\frac{6}{39} = 0.\overline{153846}$
8. $\frac{6}{15} = 0.4$
9. $\frac{57}{63} = 0.\overline{904761}$
10. $\frac{32}{36} = 0.\overline{8}$
11. $\frac{9}{36} = 0.25$
12. $\frac{45}{72} = 0.625$
13. $\frac{35}{55} = 0.\overline{63}$
14. $\frac{4}{36} = 0.\overline{1}$
15. $\frac{30}{45} = 0.\overline{6}$
16. $\frac{21}{36} = 0.58\overline{3}$
17. $\frac{56}{74} = 0.\overline{756}$
18. $\frac{12}{18} = 0.\overline{6}$
19. $\frac{56}{63} = 0.\overline{8}$
20. $\frac{7}{49} = 0.\overline{142857}$
21. $\frac{16}{72} = 0.\overline{2}$

 15 KW 1009 Pre-Algebra

Name________________________ *Decimals*

Rounding Decimals

Round 4.234 to the nearest tenth. 4.2<u>3</u>4 → 4.2

Round 42.34812 to the nearest hundredth. 42.34<u>8</u>12 → 42.35

Round to the nearest whole number.

1. 42.675 = 43
2. 29.78 = 30
3. 34.87 = 35
4. 21.098 = 21
5. 15.91 = 16
6. 78.412 = 78
7. 7.8346 = 8
8. 54.927 = 55
9. 2.72 = 3
10. 54.909 = 55
11. 1.19 = 1
12. 4.98 = 5

Round to the nearest tenth.

1. 33.897 = 33.9
2. 121.345 = 121.3
3. 32.777 = 32.8
4. 5.345 = 5.3
5. 1.908 = 1.9
6. 341.08 = 341.1
7. 1.23 = 1.2
8. 1.6578 = 1.7
9. 3.869 = 3.9
10. 41.564 = 41.6
11. 654.34 = 654.3
12. 111.111 = 111.1

Round to the nearest hundredth.

1. 212.658 = 212.66
2. 21.569 = 21.57
3. 2.6354 = 2.64
4. 241.560 = 241.56
5. 7.34587 = 7.35
6. 218.453 = 218.45
7. 12.1212 = 12.12
8. 430.234 = 430.23
9. 12.7689 = 12.77
10. 129.404 = 129.40
11. 6.435 = 6.44
12. 9.9999 = 10.00

 16 KW 1009 Pre-Algebra

Answer Key

Name______________________________ *Decimals*

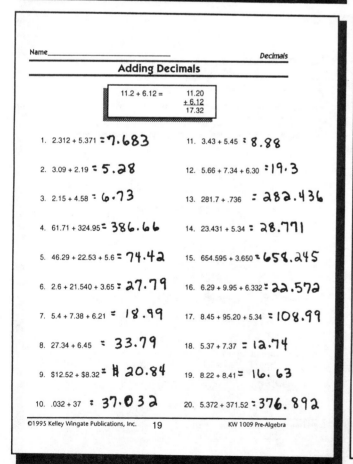

Multiplying and Dividing by 10, 100, 1000, etc.

23.76 x 10 → 23.76 → 237.6
Move the decimal point to the right one place.

23.76 x 100 → 23.76 → 2376
Move the decimal point to the right two places.

23.765 x 1000 → 23.765 → 23765
Move the decimal point to the right three places

237.6 ÷ 1000 → 237.6 → .2376
Move the decimal point to the left three places.

1. 3.456 x 10 = 34.56
2. 345.682 ÷ 100 = 3.45682
3. 3.7823 x 1000 = 3,782.3
4. 5463.23 ÷ 10,000 = 0.546323
5. 67,000 ÷ 100 = 670.00
6. .000999 x 1,000 = 0.999
7. 67.009 ÷ 1000 = 0.067009
8. 81 x 100 = 8,100
9. 23,098 ÷ 10,000 = 2.3098
11. 48.98 x 10,000 = 489,800
12. .092 ÷ 100 = 0.00092
13. .0442 x 100,000 = 4,420
14. 4.881 ÷ 100,000 = 0.00004881
15. 2.785 x 10 = 27.85
16. .0098 ÷ 100 = 0.000098
17. 4.342 x 100,000 = 434,200
18. 45,000 ÷ 1000 = 45.00
19. 2.8 x 10 = 28
20. .91 ÷ 10,000 = 0.000091
21. 32.949 x 100 = 3,294.9

Name______________________________ *Decimals*

Adding Decimals

13.3 + 7.23 = 13.30 + 7.23 = 20.53

1. 3.456 + 2.894 = 6.350
2. 4.89 + 5.73 = 10.62
3. 3.5 + 8.4 = 11.9
4. 43.56 + 105.7 = 149.26
5. 15.76 + 34.23 + 3.9 = 53.89
6. 6.8 + 13.634 + 2.34 = 22.774
7. 5.7 + 5.34 + 4.78 = 15.82
8. 12.87 + 2.87 = 15.74
9. $13.39 + $7.40 = $20.79
10. .017 + 13 = 13.017
11. 5.02 + 5.20 = 10.22
12. 9.91 + 2.734 + 8.41 = 21.054
13. 121.9 + .736 = 122.636
14. 17.438 + 4.82 = 22.258
15. 322.815 + 6.876 = 329.691
16. 5.97 + 4.87 + 3.908 = 14.748
17. 3.83 + 45.90 + 5.00 = 54.73
18. 5.94 + 5.32 = 11.26
19. 6.41 + 3.99 = 10.4
20. 2.987 + 451.90 = 454.887

Name______________________________ *Decimals*

Adding Decimals

11.2 + 6.12 = 11.20 + 6.12 = 17.32

1. 2.312 + 5.371 = 7.683
2. 3.09 + 2.19 = 5.28
3. 2.15 + 4.58 = 6.73
4. 61.71 + 324.95 = 386.66
5. 46.29 + 22.53 + 5.6 = 74.42
6. 2.6 + 21.540 + 3.65 = 27.79
7. 5.4 + 7.38 + 6.21 = 18.99
8. 27.34 + 6.45 = 33.79
9. $12.52 + $8.32 = $20.84
10. .032 + 37 = 37.032
11. 3.43 + 5.45 = 8.88
12. 5.66 + 7.34 + 6.30 = 19.3
13. 281.7 + .736 = 282.436
14. 23.431 + 5.34 = 28.771
15. 654.595 + 3.650 = 658.245
16. 6.29 + 9.95 + 6.332 = 22.572
17. 8.45 + 95.20 + 5.34 = 108.99
18. 5.37 + 7.37 = 12.74
19. 8.22 + 8.41 = 16.63
20. 5.372 + 371.52 = 376.892

Name______________________________ *Decimals*

Subtracting Decimals

17.2 - 5.10 = 17.20 − 5.10 = 12.10

1. 13.2 − 6.7 = 6.5
2. 13.3 − 12.4 = 0.9
3. 62.1 − 33.29 = 28.81
4. 76.34 − 47.30 = 29.04
5. 325.34 − 235.34 = 90.00
6. 55.23 − 47.29 = 7.94
7. $21.73 − $16.43 = $5.30
8. 3.239 − .06 = 3.179
9. 23.28 − .002 − 1.2 = 22.078
10. 35.63 − .021 = 35.609
11. 543.43 − 35.342 = 508.088
12. 436.82 − 328.56 = 108.26
13. 75.034 − 22.439 = 52.595
14. 439.02 − 232.76 = 206.26
15. 756.98 − 32.43 = 724.55
16. 65.9 − 33.32 = 32.58
17. 21.32 − 4.28 = 17.04
18. 4.64 − .476 = 4.164
19. 121.32 − 4.34 = 116.98
20. 34.32 − 12.43 = 21.89

Name________________________ *Decimals*

Subtracting Decimals

13.5 – 4.21 = 13.50 – 4.21 = 9.29

1. 4.7 – 2.3 = 2.4
2. 24.34 – 23.19 = 1.15
3. 84.87 – 78.45 = 6.42
4. 85.76 – 34.65 = 51.11
5. 342.43 – 259.24 = 83.19
6. 74.81 – 61.92 = 12.89
7. $54.68 – $23.76 = $30.92
8. 7.435 – .0345 = 7.4005
9. 43.50 – .015 – 3.2 = 40.285
10. 56.40 – .043 = 56.357
11. 756.84 – 31.343 = 725.497
12. 34245.34 – 28674.87 = 5570.47
13. 82.72 – 43.658 = 39.062
14. 954.34 – 657.56 = 296.78
15. 843.44 – 22.39 = 821.05
16. 84.8 – 44.87 = 39.93
17. 93.76 – 8.67 = 85.09
18. 6.56 – .654 = 5.906
19. 254.54 – 6.45 = 248.09
20. 39.43 – 15.34 = 24.09

Name________________________ *Decimals*

Multiplying Decimals

(.6) (.07) — 3 decimal places — .6 x .07 = .042

1. (.004) (8) = 0.032
2. (.051) (.006) = 0.000306
3. (340) (.02) = 6.8
4. (9.4) (3) = 28.2
5. (4.52) (6) = 27.12
6. (3.28) (12.8) = 41.984
7. (.016) (3.8) = 0.0608
8. (.004) (4) (.04) = 0.00064
9. (1.4) (.978) (.07) = 0.095844
10. (.05) (.17) (.002) = 0.000017
11. (.34) (.12) (.104) = 0.0042432
12. (11.9) (.02) (3.09) = 0.73542
13. (12.3) (5.81) (.06) = 4.28778
14. (4) (.112) = 0.448
15. (12.89) (.331) = 4.26659
16. (3.906) (12.12) = 47.34072
17. (2.09) (.005) = 0.01045
18. (18.92) (.4) (.32) = 2.42176
19. (.012) (6) (.05) = 0.0036
20. (8) (.342) (.02) = 0.05472

Name________________________ *Decimals*

Multiplying Decimals

(.4) (.06) — 3 decimal places — .4 x .06 = .024

Multiply. Use mental math

1. 0.06 x 0.4 = 0.024
2. (1.2) (0.03) = 0.036
3. (0.9) (0.9) = 0.81
4. 0.03 x 0.08 = 0.0024
5. 0.5 x 0.06 = 0.03
6. (0.11) (0.05) = 0.0055
7. (0.7) (0.07) = 0.049
8. 0.12 x 0.04 = 0.0048
9. (0.8) (0.005) = 0.004
10. (0.9) (0.002) (.005) = 0.0018
11. (0.012) (0.7) = 0.0084
12. (0.7) (0.011) = 0.0077
13. 0.03 x 0.6 = 0.018
14. (1.1) (0.11) = 0.121
15. (0.12) (.05) = 0.006
16. 0.06 x 0.07 = 0.0042
17. (0.10) (0.05) = 0.005
18. (0.012) (1.2) = 0.0144
19. (0.6) (0.8) = 0.48
20. (0.02) (1.2) = 0.024

Name________________________ *Decimals*

Dividing Decimals

.0173613 ÷ .33 =

```
      .05261
33 )01.73613
     165
      186
       66
      201
      198
        33
        33
         0
```

1. 12.63 ÷ .9 = $14.0\overline{3}$
2. 3.56 ÷ 2.5 = 1.424
3. 9.434 ÷ 3.03 = $3.1\overline{1353}$
4. 42.78 ÷ .187 = 228.77005
5. 8.3096 ÷ 5.2 = 1.598
6. 1.35 ÷ .07 = $19.\overline{285714}$
7. 12.257 ÷ 5.8 = 2.1132758
8. 3.908 ÷ 3.2 = 1.221125
9. 7.76 ÷ 1.2 = $6.4\overline{6}$
10. 6.56 ÷ .16 = 41
11. .0135 ÷ 4.5 = 0.003
12. .483 ÷ .22 = $2.19\overline{54}$
13. 9.414 ÷ 3.3 = $2.85\overline{27}$
14. 16.73 ÷ .12 = $139.41\overline{6}$
15. .1927 ÷ .0543 = 3.5488029
16. 9.54 ÷ 3.03 = $3.\overline{1485}$

Answer Key

Name____________________________ *Decimals*

Dividing Decimals

Divide. Use mental math.

1. 0.36 ÷ 0.4 = 0.9
2. 5.4 ÷ 0.06 = 90
3. 1.21 ÷ 0.11 = 11
4. 1.69 ÷ 0.13 = 13
5. 0.032 ÷ 0.4 = 0.08
6. 9.6 ÷ 0.12 = 80
7. 14.4 ÷ 1.2 = 12
8. 0.012 ÷ 0.3 = .04
9. 0.56 ÷ 0.008 = 70
10. 0.072 ÷ 0.08 = 0.9
11. 2.6 ÷ 0.02 = 130
12. 0.55 ÷ 0.005 = 110
13. 0.0027 ÷ 0.9 = 0.003
14. 100 ÷ 0.01 = 10,000
15. 0.132 ÷ 0.012 = 11
16. 7.2 ÷ 0.06 = 120
17. 0.064 ÷ 0.8 = 0.08
18. 0.0054 ÷ 0.006 = 0.9
19. 3.6 ÷ 0.009 = 400
20. 0.24 ÷ 0.008 = 30
21. 84 ÷ 1.2 = 70
22. 0.108 ÷ 0.09 = 1.2

Name____________________________ *Decimals*

Practice with Decimals

1. 2.62 ÷ .54 = 4.851
2. 31.25 + 23.5 = 54.75
3. (9.9) (2.03) = 20.097
4. 8726 ÷ 2.84 = 3072.5352
5. 1.32 ÷ 1.22 = 1.0819672
6. 6.55 + .08 = 6.63
7. 12.78 – 7.2 = 5.58
8. (3.2) (4.065) = 13.008
9. 21.7 – 15.9 = 5.8
10. .6 + .09 + 1.75 = 2.44
11. (2.5) (3.4) (4.4) = 37.4
12. 87.21 –23.98 + 11.12 = 74.35
13. (.03) (.23) (1.3) = 0.00897
14. 23.65 ÷ 22.81 = 1.0368259
15. 2.34 ÷ .983 = 2.3804679
16. 65.78 + 54.90 = 120.68
17. 432.42 – 237.89 = 194.53
18. 12.938 + 11.548 = 24.486
19. 789.987 – 231.093 = 558.894
20. (13.2) (34.9) = 460.68
21. 1243.32 – 1032.90 = 210.42
22. 5.23 ÷ 3.12 = 1.676282

Name____________________________ *Decimals*

Practice with Decimals

1. 3.56 ÷ .73 = 4.8767123
2. 22.59 + 33.5 = 56.09
3. (4.3) (3.59) = 15.437
4. 3496 ÷ 3.549 = 985.06621
5. 7.459 ÷ 2.459 = 3.0333468
6. 7.546 + .0958 = 7.6418
7. 15.54 – 8.34 = 7.2
8. (6.5) (5.304) = 34.476
9. 43.7 – 34.5 = 9.2
10. .8 + .07 + 3.73 = 4.6
11. (5.5) (2.6) (4.0) = 57.2
12. 33.54 –22.56 + 23.43 = 34.41
13. (2.3) (3.04) (3.46) = 24.19232
14. 84.34 ÷ 65.76 = 1.2825425
15. 4.33 ÷ .393 = 11.017811
16. 54.34 + 31.98 = 86.32
17. 843.21 – 342.03 = 501.18
18. 23.434 + 23.403 = 46.837
19. 345.765 – 237.405 = 108.36
20. (23.4) (3.9) = 91.26
21. 1465.65 – 1253.42 = 212.23
22. 6.37 ÷ 6.50 = 0.98

Name____________________________ *Decimals*

Problem Solving With Decimals

Marilyn and Mackie decided to go the the beach. They went to a grocery store and bought some sandwiches for $5.67, a gallon of fruit punch for $2.31, and a bag of potato chips for $1.21. How much did they spend altogether?

$5.67 + $2.31 + $1.21=

$5.67	each grocery item
$2.31	
+$1.21	
$9.19	total

1. Wilson and Linda went to the dress store to buy Linda a new dress. The dress that Linda picked out costs $95.00. If the price was reduced by $13.68, how much will Linda pay? $ 81.32
2. Norman's credit card bill was $23.43 for January, $65.98 for February, and $21.90 for March. What were his total charges for the first three months of the year? $ 111.31
3. Faith went to her favorite store and bought a sweater for $82.95. She then went to a shoe store and bought a pair of shoes for $87.34. How much money did Faith spend altogether? $ 170.29
4. Lamar loves to go fishing. Before his last trip he decided to buy a few more peces of equipment. he bought a tackle box for $23.98, a fishing pole for $54.93, a life jacket for $34.21, and an ice chest for $121.28. How much did Lamar spend altogether? $ 234.40
5. Nancy and Kathy decided to make a quilt instead of buying one. The materials for the quilt totaled $45.87. The cost of a new quilt is $78.98. How much money did they save? $ 33.11
6. Joann loves to shop. On her last shoppping trip she bought a dress for $34.90, a pair of shoes for $89.09, a hat for $65.99, a coat for $34.21, and a belt for $12.99. How much did Joann spend altogether? $ 237.18

Answer Key

Name______________________ *Decimals*

Changing Decimals to Fractions

Terminating Decimals	Repeating Decimals
$.50 = \frac{50}{100} = \frac{1}{2}$	$x = .\overline{33} = .3333...$
	$100x = 33.3333...$
$.120 = \frac{120}{1000} = \frac{3}{25}$	$-\quad x = -\ .3333...$
	$\frac{99x}{99} = \frac{33}{99}$
	$x = \frac{1}{3}$
	or $.\overline{33} = \frac{1}{3}$

1. $.36 = \frac{9}{25}$
2. $.91\overline{6} = \frac{11}{12}$
3. $.625 = \frac{5}{8}$
4. $.55 = \frac{11}{20}$
5. $.\overline{46} = \frac{46}{99}$
6. $.\overline{33} = \frac{1}{3}$
7. $.3\overline{8} = \frac{7}{18}$
8. $.775 = \frac{31}{40}$
9. $.6875 = \frac{11}{16}$
10. $.5625 = \frac{9}{16}$
11. $.\overline{27} = \frac{3}{11}$
12. $.212 = \frac{53}{250}$

Name______________________ *Decimals*

Changing Decimals to Fractions

1. $.345 = \frac{69}{200}$
2. $.1\overline{34} = \frac{133}{990}$
3. $.942 = \frac{471}{500}$
4. $.5\overline{48} = \frac{181}{330}$
5. $.438 = \frac{219}{500}$
6. $.34 = \frac{17}{50}$
7. $.506 = \frac{253}{500}$
8. $.65 = \frac{13}{20}$
9. $.166 = \frac{83}{500}$
10. $.9\overline{33} = \frac{84}{90}$
11. $.229 = \frac{229}{1000}$
12. $.129 = \frac{129}{1000}$
13. $.333 = \frac{333}{1000}$
14. $.243 = \frac{243}{1000}$
15. $.28 = \frac{7}{25}$
16. $.59 = \frac{59}{100}$
17. $.342 = \frac{171}{500}$
18. $.7\overline{34} = \frac{727}{990}$
19. $.930 = \frac{93}{100}$
20. $.777 = \frac{777}{1000}$
21. $.819 = \frac{819}{1000}$
22. $.378 = \frac{189}{500}$

Name______________________ *Ratios, Proportions and Percents*

Ratios

4 to 12 → $\frac{4}{12} = \frac{1}{3}$

25 :35 → $\frac{25}{35} = \frac{5}{7}$

5 out of 20 → $\frac{5}{20} = \frac{1}{4}$

1. 88 to 40 $= \frac{88}{40} = \frac{11}{5}$
2. 110 : 112 $= \frac{110}{112} = \frac{55}{56}$
3. 21 out of 84 $= \frac{21}{84} = \frac{1}{4}$
4. 197 to 17 $= \frac{197}{17}$
5. 18 to 76 $= \frac{18}{76} = \frac{9}{38}$
6. .11 : 1.21 $= \frac{.11}{1.21} = \frac{1}{11}$
7. 130 to 112 $= \frac{130}{112} = \frac{65}{56}$
8. 65 out of 115 $= \frac{65}{115} = \frac{13}{23}$
9. 19 out of 27 $= \frac{19}{27}$
10. 65 : 35 $= \frac{65}{35} = \frac{13}{7}$
11. 113 : 226 $= \frac{113}{226} = \frac{1}{2}$
12. 30 out of 323 $= \frac{30}{323}$
13. 40 out of 80 $= \frac{40}{80} = \frac{1}{2}$
14. 167 to 132 $= \frac{167}{132} =$
15. 175 to 200 $= \frac{175}{200} = \frac{7}{8}$
16. 77 : 177 $= \frac{77}{177}$

Name______________________ *Ratios, Proportions and Percents*

Ratios

3 to 9 → $\frac{3}{9} = \frac{1}{3}$

45 :25 → $\frac{45}{25} = \frac{9}{5}$

6 out of 36 → $\frac{6}{36} = \frac{1}{6}$

1. 21 to 45 $= \frac{21}{45} = \frac{7}{15}$
2. 121 : 108 $= \frac{121}{108}$
3. 34 out of 82 $= \frac{34}{82} = \frac{17}{41}$
4. 237 to 32 $= \frac{237}{32}$
5. 19 to 84 $= \frac{19}{84}$
6. .10 : 1.40 $= \frac{.10}{1.40} = \frac{1}{14}$
7. 60 to 116 $= \frac{60}{116} = \frac{15}{29}$
8. 12 out of 133 $= \frac{12}{133}$
9. 14 out of 43 $= \frac{14}{43}$
10. 25 : 75 $= \frac{1}{3}$
11. 112 : 224 $= \frac{112}{224} = \frac{1}{2}$
12. 40 out of 231 $= \frac{40}{231}$
13. 30 out of 90 $= \frac{30}{90} = \frac{1}{3}$
14. 171 to 132 $= \frac{171}{132} = \frac{57}{44}$
15. 150 to 225 $= \frac{150}{225} = \frac{2}{3}$
16. 52 : 104 $= \frac{52}{104} = \frac{1}{2}$

Answer Key

Name____________________________ *Ratios, Proportions and Percents*

Proportions

$$\frac{4}{6} = \frac{x}{36}$$
$$4 \cdot 36 = 6x$$
$$\frac{144}{6} = \frac{6x}{6}$$
$$24 = x$$

1. $\frac{16}{48} = \frac{x}{100}$ $x = 33\frac{1}{3}$
2. $\frac{18}{24} = \frac{12}{p}$ $p = 16$
3. $\frac{6}{6} = \frac{6x}{6}$ $x = 1$
4. $\frac{1.8}{d} = \frac{3.6}{2.8}$ $d = 1.4$
5. $\frac{8}{h} = \frac{5}{2}$ $h = 3\frac{1}{5}$
6. $\frac{144}{6} = \frac{6x}{6}$ $x = 24$
7. $\frac{20}{30} = \frac{10}{x}$ $x = 15$
8. $\frac{4}{5} = \frac{x}{5}$ $x = 4$
9. $\frac{.14}{.07} = \frac{v}{1.5}$ $v = 3$
10. $\frac{80}{z} = \frac{48}{20}$ $z = 33\frac{1}{3}$
11. $\frac{18}{45} = \frac{2}{c}$ $c = 5$
12. $\frac{8}{6} = \frac{w}{27}$ $w = 36$
13. $\frac{1}{3} = \frac{x}{6}$ $x = 2$
14. $\frac{24}{12} = \frac{x}{6}$ $x = 12$
15. $\frac{6}{t} = \frac{6}{4}$ $t = 4$
16. $\frac{r}{3} = \frac{8}{8}$ $r = 3$

Name____________________________ *Ratios, Proportions and Percents*

Problems Using Proportions

If 2 liters of orange juice cost 2.50, how much do 7 liters cost?

$$\frac{2}{2.50} = \frac{7}{x}$$
$$2x = 2.50 \cdot 7$$
$$\frac{2x}{2} = \frac{17.50}{2} \qquad x = 8.75$$

7 liters cost \$8.75

1. If 2 meters of fabric costs \$3.45, what should 7 meters cost? \$12.08
2. A 16 ounce box of laundry detergent costs \$2.49. How many ounces should be in a box marked \$1.15? 7.4 oz.
3. Three pounds of chicken costs \$3.67. How much should 15 pounds cost? \$18.35
4. If 7 ounces of cola costs \$.59. How much should 19 ounces cost? \$1.60
5. Judy and Tomie traveled 237 hours in 8 hours. If they continue traveling at the same rate, how long will it take them to travel 654 miles? 22 hrs.
6. Neil ran 5.5 miles in 1 hour. If he continues running at the same pace, how far will he have run in 7.25 hours? 39.88 mi.
7. Marty and Lance saw an advertisement for a 24 pound bag of oranges that costs \$5.98. How much should a 13 pound bag cost? \$3.24
8. If a 12 pound turkey costs \$24.98, what should 20 pounds cost? \$41.63
9. 12 ounces of fish cost \$4.21. How much should 23 ounces cost? \$8.07

Name____________________________ *Ratios, Proportions and Percents*

Percents

Fraction to percent	Decimal to percent
$\frac{1}{2} \rightarrow \frac{1}{2} = \frac{x}{100}$	$.535 \rightarrow .535 = 53.5\%$
$100 = 2x$ $50 = x$ $\frac{1}{2} = 50\%$	***When converting a decimal to a percent, move the decimal 2 places to the right.***

Write each expresion as a percent.

1. $\frac{5}{46}$ = 10.87%
2. 2.392 = 239.2%
3. 2.3838 = 238.38%
4. $\frac{7}{15}$ = 46.7%
5. 3.293 = 329.3%
6. 17.3839 = 1738.39%
7. 11.6 = 1160%
8. 412.32 = 41232%
9. $\frac{12}{17}$ = 70.59%
10. $\frac{11}{23}$ = 47.83%
11. 4.34 = 434%
12. $\frac{4}{13}$ = 30.77%

Name____________________________ *Ratios, Proportions and Percents*

Percents

80%
$$80\% = \frac{80}{100} = \frac{8}{10} = \frac{4}{5}$$

51.5%
$$51.5\% = \frac{51.5}{100} = \frac{515}{1000} = \frac{21}{40}$$

Write each percent as a fraction and each fraction as a percent.

1. $4\frac{5}{46}$ = 410.9%
2. 8.6% = $\frac{43}{500}$
3. 4.934% = $\frac{2467}{50,000}$
4. $4\frac{5}{46}$ = 410.9%
5. .98% = $\frac{49}{5000}$
6. 564.89% = $\frac{56489}{10,000}$
7. 12.4% = $\frac{31}{250}$
8. 5.75% = $\frac{23}{400}$
9. 23.7% = $\frac{237}{1000}$
10. 21.98% = $\frac{1099}{5000}$
11. $7\frac{4}{23}$ = 717.4%
12. $3\frac{56}{77}$ = 372.7%
13. 2.98% = $\frac{149}{5000}$
14. $21\frac{7}{32}$ = 2121.9%
15. $6\frac{1}{2}$ = 650%
16. $2\frac{5}{7}$ = 271%

Answer Key

Name________________________ *Ratios, Proportions and Percents*

Percents

50% of 40 = ______	____% of 20 = 10	40% of ______ = 20
$\frac{50}{100} = \frac{x}{40}$	$\frac{x}{100} = \frac{10}{20}$	$\frac{40}{100} = \frac{20}{x}$
100x = 2000	20x = 1000	40x = 2000
x = 20	x = 50 50%	x = 50

1. 20% of 12 = 2.4
2. 30% of 80 = 24
3. 16% of 85 = 13.6
4. 17% of 65 = 11.05
5. 45% of 50 = 22.5
6. 60 % of 25 = 15
7. 25 % of 40 = 10
8. 16.7 % of 48 = 8
9. 50.8 % of 65 = 33
10. 44.4 % of 9 = 4
11. 34% of 100 = 34
12. 67% of 119.4 = 80
13. 20% of 375 = 75
14. 45% of 266.7 = 120
15. 12% of 633.3 = 76
16. 60% of 73.3 = 44

Name________________________ *Ratios, Proportions and Percents*

Problems With Percents

A baseball team played 50 games. They won 50% of them. How many games did the team win?

50% of 50 = _____

$\frac{50}{100} = \frac{x}{50}$

100x = 250

x = 25

1. In a group of 50 children, 18 have red shirts. What percent have red shirts? 36%
2. A test had 80 questions. Diane got 90% of them correct. How many problems did Diane get correct? 72
3. A soccer team played 32 games. They won 25% of them. how many games did the team win? 8 games
4. The regular price of a blouse is $34.00. Find the amount of the discount and the reduced price if there is a 30% discount. $10.20 discount / $23.80 price
5. A puppy weighed 4.5 pounds at 5 weeks and 7.5 pounds at 8 weeks. What was the percent increase? 66.7%
6. Sam went to a restaurant and decided to give the waiter a 15% tip. If the bill is $13.50, how much should Sam tip the waiter? $2.03
7. John bought a new computer that costs $85.00. The printer is 13% of the purchase price. Find the total cost including the printer. $96.05
8. Sugar-free gum contains 40% less calories than regular gum. If a piece of regular gum contains 40 calories, how may calories does a piece of sugar-free gum contain? 24 calories

Name________________________ *Integers*

Adding Integers with Like Signs

5 + 6 = 11 (positive)	-4 + -11 = -15 (negative)
2 positives	2 negatives

1. 5 + 6 = 11
2. -12 + -7 = -19
3. 32 + 53 = 85
4. -34 + -76 = -110
5. 142 + 374 = 516
6. -42 + -38 = -80
7. 45 + 8 = 53
8. -61 + -39 = -100
9. 23 + 72 = 95
10. -17 + -17 = -34
11. 90 + 52 = 142
12. -13 + -34 + -67 = -114
13. 23 + 45 + 65 = 133
14. -43 + -36 + -21 = -100
15. 13 + 45 + 84 = 142
16. -16 + -16 + -16 = -48
17. 15 + 41 + 7 = 63
18. -2 + -124 + -438 = -564
19. 12 + 45 + 396 = 453
20. -12 + -37 + -48 + -361 = -458

Name________________________ *Integers*

Adding Integers with Like Signs

7 + 7 = 14 (positive)	-6 + -12 = -18 (negative)
2 positives	2 negatives

1. 7 + 8 = 15
2. -14 + -9 = -23
3. 47 + 93 = 140
4. -21 + -34 = -55
5. 213 + 375 = 588
6. -163 + -538 = -701
7. 28 + 67 = 95
8. -12 + -68 = -80
9. 34 + 46 = 80
10. -23 + -48 = -71
11. 70 + 82 = 152
12. -21 + -22 + -41 = -84
13. 54 + 63 + 82 = 199
14. -21 + -41 + -55 = -117
15. 36 + 57 + 58 = 151
16. -18 + -34 + -59 = -111
17. 21 + 22 + 23 = 66
18. -21 + -59 + -828 = -908
19. 51 + 87 + 527 = 665
20. -13 + -67 + -78 + -832 = -990

Answer Key

Name________________________ *Integers*

Adding Integers with Unlike Signs

sign
15 + [-26] = -11
[26 − 15]

sign
-13 + [27] = 14
[27 − 13]

Find each sum.

1. 8 + -9 = -1
2. -18 + 6 = -12
3. 56 + -7 = 49
4. -17 + 33 = 16
5. -213 + 56 = -157
6. -167 + 121 = -46
7. 48 + -56 = -8
8. -61 + 61 = 0
9. 672 + -423 = 249
10. -19 + 39 = 20
11. -73 + 42 = -31
12. 419 + -673 = -254
13. -2,895 + 576 = -2,319
14. 17,985 + -33,789 = -15,804
15. 45,908 + -12,921 = 32,987
16. -563,937 + 76,412 = -487,525
17. -12 + 9 = -3
18. 46 + -34 = 12
19. 57 + -90 = -33
20. -87,121 + 86,323 = -798

Name________________________ *Integers*

Adding Integers with Unlike Signs

sign
57 + [-67] = -10
[67 − 57]

sign
-16 + [29] = 13
[29 − 16]

Find each sum.

1. 34 + -78 = -44
2. -194 + 635 = 441
3. 321 + -393 = -72
4. -43 + 68 = 25
5. -343 + 439 = 96
6. -595 + 630 = 35
7. 88 + -34 = 54
8. -99 + 94 = -5
9. 850 + -828 = 22
10. -73 + 29 = -44
11. -6,907 + 4,262 = -2,645
12. 713 + -6,976 = -6,263
13. -23,895 + 5,863 = -18,032
14. 232,985 + -454,202 = -221,217
15. 67,999 + -78,952 = -10,953
16. -112,956 + 565,453 = 452,497
17. -65,908 + 73,912 = 8,004
18. 57,980 + -41,978 = 16,002
19. 57,908 + -84,512 = -26,604
20. -84,154 + 89,343 = 5,189

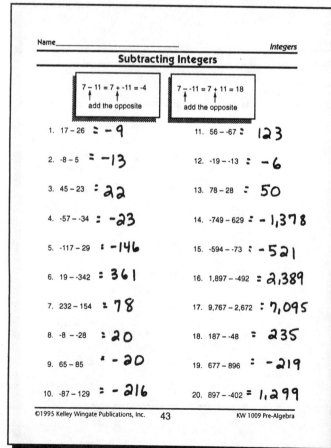

Name________________________ *Integers*

Subtracting Integers

7 − 11 = 7 + -11 = -4
add the opposite

7 − -11 = 7 + 11 = 18
add the opposite

1. 17 − 26 = -9
2. -8 − 5 = -13
3. 45 − 23 = 22
4. -57 − -34 = -23
5. -117 − 29 = -146
6. 19 − -342 = 361
7. 232 − 154 = 78
8. -8 − -28 = 20
9. 65 − 85 = -20
10. -87 − 129 = -216
11. 56 − -67 = 123
12. -19 − -13 = -6
13. 78 − 28 = 50
14. -749 − 629 = -1,378
15. -594 − -73 = -521
16. 1,897 − -492 = 2,389
17. 9,767 − 2,672 = 7,095
18. 187 − -48 = 235
19. 677 − 896 = -219
20. 897 − -402 = 1,299

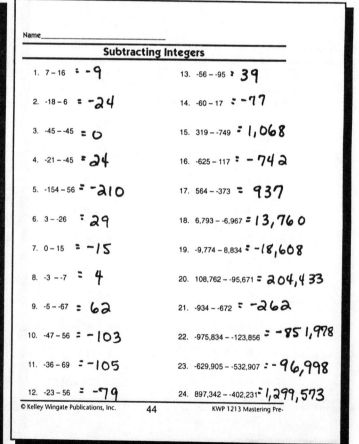

Name________________________

Subtracting Integers

1. 7 − 16 = -9
2. -18 − 6 = -24
3. -45 − -45 = 0
4. -21 − -45 = 24
5. -154 − 56 = -210
6. 3 − -26 = 29
7. 0 − 15 = -15
8. -3 − -7 = 4
9. -5 − -67 = 62
10. -47 − 56 = -103
11. -36 − 69 = -105
12. -23 − 56 = -79
13. -56 − -95 = 39
14. -60 − 17 = -77
15. 319 − -749 = 1,068
16. -625 − 117 = -742
17. 564 − -373 = 937
18. 6,793 − -6,967 = 13,760
19. -9,774 − 8,834 = -18,608
20. 108,762 − -95,671 = 204,433
21. -934 − -672 = -262
22. -975,834 − -123,856 = -851,978
23. -629,905 − -532,907 = -96,998
24. 897,342 − -402,231 = 1,299,573

Answer Key

Name________________________ *Integers*

Adding & Subtracting Integers

1. -8 + -9 = -17
2. -10 – 4 = -14
3. -15 + 20 = 5
4. 31 – -8 = 39
5. -17 + 9 = -8
6. -9 – -26 = 17
7. -78 – 65 = -143
8. 13 + -7 = 6
9. 113 – -62 = 175
10. 0 – -9 = 9
11. 34 + -68 = -34
12. 608 – 343 = 265
13. -24 – -38 = 14
14. 0 – 17 = -17
15. -56 – 45 = -101
16. 73 + -18 = 55
17. -232 – -232 = 0
18. -108 + -676 = -784
19. 43 + -56 – 78 = -91
20. -98 – -126 + 19 = 47
21. 91 – 176 – -11 = -74
22. -17 + 436 + -642 = -223
23. -121 + -732 – -13 = -840
24. -534 – -454 + -78 = -158

Name________________________ *Integers*

Multiplying Integers

(3) (2) = 6 (-2) (-4) = 8
+ + = + - - = +
Like signs–Positive

(-3) (2) = -6 (2) (-4) = 8
- + = - + - = -
Unlike signs–Negative

1. (-3) (9) = -27
2. (15) (-4) = -60
3. (35) (3) = 105
4. (32) (-48) = -1,536
5. (56) (12) = 672
6. (-76) (43) = -3,268
7. (-39) (-58) = 2,262
8. (-323) (-10) = 3,230
9. (37) (-90) = -3,330
10. (-11) (-11) = 121
11. (-19) (-10) (2) (3) = 1,140
12. (-5) (-28) (-23) = -3,220
13. (12) (-28) = -336
14. (33) (-123) (12) = -48,708
15. (14) (-33) (2) = -924
16. (20) (-3) (23) (-3) = 4,140
17. (12) (-12) (2) (-44) = 12,672
18. (121) (-10) (21) = -25,410
19. (-9) (-88) (-7) = -5,544
20. (-32) (-33) (-34) = -35,904

Name________________________ *Integers*

Multiplying Integers

1. (5) (-4) (-2) = 40
2. (-8) (-9) = 72
3. (-7) (-3) = 21
4. (-12) (-5) (-3) = -180
5. (-6) (-2) (-5) = -60
6. (-29) (-2) = 58
7. (21) (-22) = -462
8. (43) (111) (-1) = -4,773
9. (-5) (-100) (-302) = -151,000
10. (-66) (213) = -14,058
11. (-9) (-88) (-7) = -5,544
12. (-2) (-14) (-4) = -112
13. (-6) (-9) = 54
14. (8) (-103) (-77) (-22) = -1,395,856
15. (-7) (-14) (121) = 11,858
16. (-1) (22) (-33) (44) = 31,944
17. (-85) (-219) = 18,615
18. (213) (4) (18) = 15,336
19. (-19) (-38) (-26) = -18,772
20. (1) (-42) (-6) = 252

Name________________________ *Integers*

Dividing Integers

$\frac{-27}{-9}$ = 3
- ÷ - = +
Like signs–Positive

49 ÷ -6 = -8
+ ÷ - = -
Unlike signs–negative

1. 200 ÷ -4 = -50
2. -60 ÷ 3 = -20
3. 120 ÷ -6 = -20
4. 84 ÷ -21 = -4
5. -188 ÷ 4 = -47
6. 144 ÷ -12 = -12
7. 80 ÷ -5 = -16
8. 72 ÷ 4 = 18
9. -36 ÷ 6 = -6
10. -150 ÷ 6 = -25
11. $\frac{-18}{-18}$ = 1
12. $\frac{-104}{8}$ = -13
13. $\frac{27}{-9}$ = -3
14. $\frac{-77}{7}$ = -11
15. $\frac{147}{21}$ = 7
16. $\frac{-50}{-5}$ = 10
17. $\frac{220}{-10}$ = -22
18. $\frac{168}{-14}$ = -12
19. $\frac{-288}{-12}$ = 24
20. $\frac{-30}{3}$ = -10

Answer Key

Name________________ *Integers*

Dividing Integers

1. -13 ÷ 13 = -1
2. 60 ÷ -10 = -6
3. -72 ÷ 9 = -8
4. -160 ÷ -40 = 4
5. -150 ÷ 6 = -25
6. -130 ÷ -65 = 2
7. -54 ÷ -9 = 6
8. -147 ÷ -21 = 7
9. 75 ÷ -3 = -25
10. -125 ÷ 5 = -25
11. -90 ÷ 2 = -45
12. -210 ÷ -5 = 42
13. $\frac{-66}{-11}$ = 6
14. $\frac{-655}{-5}$ = 131
15. $\frac{-80}{10}$ = -8
16. $\frac{-72}{8}$ = -9
17. $\frac{-35}{-7}$ = 5
18. $\frac{-468}{26}$ = -18
19. $\frac{-253}{11}$ = -23
20. $\frac{66}{-2}$ = -33
21. $\frac{-84}{-7}$ = 12
22. $\frac{258}{-3}$ = -86
23. $\frac{-310}{5}$ = -62
24. $\frac{-552}{23}$ = -24

©1995 Kelley Wingate Publications, Inc. 49 KW 1009 Pre-Algebra

Name________________ *Integers*

Mixed Practice with Integers

1. -34 + -122 = -156
2. 80 − -22 = 102
3. -3 • 5 = -15
4. 19 • -23 = -437
5. 83 + -85 = -2
6. 28 − -65 = 93
7. 28 − -26 = 54
8. -31 − -21 = -10
9. -35 + 62 + -90 = -63
10. 12 • -13 • 6 = -936
11. (212 + -234 − 222) ÷ -6 = $40\frac{2}{3}$
12. 100 • 3 • 21 = 6,300
13. $\frac{175}{-5}$ • -4 = 140
14. $\frac{-555}{-5}$ • -6 = -666
15. $\frac{-424}{4}$ = -106
16. $\frac{-72}{8} + \frac{-64}{6} + \frac{33}{-11}$ = $-22\frac{2}{3}$
17. (225 ÷ 5) • .2 = 9
18. (-19 − -21 − -34) ÷ -6 = -6
19. (-18 − -77 − 22) • 2 = 74
20. (10 + -31 + -80) ÷ 3 = $-33\frac{2}{3}$
21. (16 − 21 + 34) ÷ -8 = $-3\frac{5}{8}$
22. (-320 + -75 + 24) • 4 = -1,484
23. (-12 + 13 + 55) • 3 = 168
24. (-12 − 54 − 10) • 2 = -152

©1995 Kelley Wingate Publications, Inc. 50 KW 1009 Pre-Algebra

Name________________ *Integers*

Problem Solving With Integers

1. A helicopter started at 0 feet. At takeoff it rose 2100 feet. It then decended 600 feet because the pilot wanted to take a photograph. A flock of birds ws appraoching so the helicopter rose 3200 feet. After the approaching flock of birds passed, the helicopter decended 2600 feet. How high was the helicopter flying after the last decent? 2,100 ft.
2. Cindy goes to school in a 7-story building. Her first class is on the first floor. She goes up 3 floors for her second class and down 2 floors for her third class. For her fourth class Cindy goes up five floors and for her final class Cindy goes down 1 floor. What floor is Cindy on during her final class? 6th floor
3. Some number added to -12 is 36. Add this number to -15. Then multiply this number by -2. What is the final number? -66
4. Some number subtracted by -6 is 41. Multiply this number by -3. Then divide this number by -4. What is the final number? $26\frac{1}{4}$
5. A bus driver started her day with an empty bus. At her first stop she picked up 11 people. At her second stop she picked up 5 more people and let 7 people get off. At her third stop she picked up 5 people and let 2 off. How many people were on the bus as the driver left the third stop? 12 people
6. Some number added to -13 is 44. Divide this number by 2. Then multiply by 8. What is the final number? 228
7. Jim got a job at a ski resort. He was in charge of determining how deep the was. On the first day of the snow season it snowed 1 meter.The next day was warmer and .5 meters of the snow melted. On the second day it snowed 2 meters in the morning but by noon 1 meter had melted. How deep was the snow at noon? 1.5 meters
8. The library started the year with 14,341 books. At the end of the first week 1456 books had been checked out. At the end of the second week 3,298 books had been checked out and 2,192 books had been returned. How many books were in the library at the end of the second week? 11,779 books

©1995 Kelley Wingate Publications, Inc. 51 KW 1009 Pre-Algebra

Name________________ *Rational Numbers*

Adding and Subtracting Rational Numbers

$-4 + -2 + 2\frac{1}{2} = -6 + 2\frac{1}{2} = -5\frac{2}{2} + 2\frac{1}{2} = -3\frac{1}{2}$

1. $5\frac{1}{5} + -4.34 - 6\frac{1}{3}$ = $-5\frac{71}{150}$
2. $-2 + 6\frac{1}{5} + -4\frac{1}{3}$ = $-\frac{2}{15}$
3. $-1\frac{2}{3} + -6\frac{5}{11} + 7\frac{2}{3}$ = $-\frac{5}{11}$
4. $5\frac{5}{12} + -6.44 - 14.69$ = $-15\frac{107}{150}$
5. $-1 + -2\frac{1}{3} + -7\frac{3}{5}$ = $-10\frac{14}{15}$
6. $2\frac{5}{7} - -3\frac{6}{9} + \frac{1}{8}$ = $6\frac{85}{168}$
7. $17 - 12.2 + -9\frac{2}{5}$ = -4.6
8. 13.23 − -31.73 = 44.96
9. $12.52 - -7\frac{2}{3} + 18\frac{1}{4}$ = $38\frac{131}{300}$
10. $7\frac{1}{7} - -9.33 + 7\frac{4}{7}$ = $24\frac{31}{700}$
11. $-6 - 2\frac{3}{5} + -7\frac{2}{5}$ = -16
12. $-5\frac{2}{3} - -6\frac{1}{5} + 1\frac{7}{12}$ = $2\frac{7}{60}$
13. $7\frac{4}{13} + -9.21 - 16.32$ = $-18\frac{289}{1300}$
14. $-3 + -3\frac{1}{4} - -3\frac{3}{7}$ = $-2\frac{23}{28}$
15. $5\frac{5}{8} - -9\frac{2}{3} - \frac{2}{9}$ = $15\frac{5}{72}$
16. $12 + 13.3 + -9\frac{1}{6}$ = $16\frac{2}{15}$
17. 4.38 + -4.38 = 0
18. $17.65 + -8\frac{1}{7} + 19\frac{5}{9}$ = $29\frac{79}{1260}$

©1995 Kelley Wingate Publications, Inc. 52 KW 1009 Pre-Algebra

Answer Key

Name____________________ *Rational Numbers*

Adding and Subtracting Rational Numbers

1. $3\frac{2}{3} + -2.25 - 7\frac{2}{4} = -6\frac{1}{12}$
2. $-6 - 7\frac{3}{4} + -2\frac{2}{3} = -16\frac{5}{12}$
3. $-8\frac{1}{2} + -2\frac{4}{12} - 8\frac{1}{3} = -19\frac{1}{6}$
4. $6\frac{1}{10} + -3.25 - 12.65 = -9.8$
5. $-2 - -3\frac{1}{8} + -4\frac{3}{4} = -3\frac{5}{8}$
6. $7\frac{2}{3} - -1\frac{2}{3} + \frac{2}{3} = 10$
7. $12 - 17.3 + -3\frac{2}{3} = -8\frac{29}{30}$
8. $-11.08 - -12.67 = 1.59$
9. $19.22 - -5\frac{3}{4} + 13\frac{2}{3} = 38\frac{191}{300}$
10. $13\frac{2}{5} - 17.8 + 13\frac{4}{5} = 9\frac{2}{5}$
11. $3\frac{7}{10} + -4.23 - 7\frac{3}{8} = -7\frac{181}{200}$
12. $5\frac{2}{7} + -3.43 - 8\frac{3}{11} = -6\frac{3211}{7700}$
13. $-8 - 1\frac{3}{5} + -6\frac{1}{8} = -15\frac{29}{40}$
14. $-2\frac{3}{7} + -9\frac{6}{10} - 5\frac{2}{3} = -17\frac{73}{105}$
15. $3\frac{1}{15} + -4.38 - 13.47 = -14\frac{47}{60}$
16. $-5 - -7\frac{3}{7} + -2\frac{5}{8} = -\frac{11}{56}$
17. $3\frac{1}{2} - -6\frac{1}{3} - \frac{3}{5} = 9\frac{7}{30}$
18. $17 - 12.2 - -8\frac{4}{9} = 13\frac{11}{45}$
19. $-5.23 + 3.33 = -1.9$
20. $11.62 + -8\frac{6}{7} - 18\frac{1}{9} = -15\frac{1097}{3150}$
21. $17\frac{8}{9} - 12.2 + 16\frac{2}{7} = 21\frac{307}{315}$
22. $9\frac{2}{3} - -5.61 - 9\frac{1}{5} = 6\frac{23}{300}$

Name____________________ *Rational Numbers*

Multiplying and Dividing Rational Numbers

$3 \cdot 6 \cdot \frac{1}{3} = 18 \cdot \frac{1}{3} = \frac{\cancel{18}^{6}}{1} \cdot \frac{1}{\cancel{3}_{1}} = 6$

$2\frac{1}{3} \cdot 1\frac{3}{4} \div 1\frac{1}{2} = \frac{7}{3} \cdot \frac{7}{4} \div \frac{3}{2} = \frac{7}{3} \cdot \frac{7}{\cancel{4}_{2}} \cdot \frac{\cancel{2}^{1}}{3} = \frac{98}{9}$ or $10\frac{8}{9}$

1. $2\frac{2}{3} \cdot -6\frac{1}{5} = -16\frac{8}{15}$
2. $-4 \cdot 2\frac{1}{5} \cdot -7\frac{1}{3} = 64\frac{8}{15}$
3. $-9\frac{2}{3} \cdot 3\frac{7}{12} = -34\frac{23}{36}$
4. $1\frac{5}{12} \cdot 3.29 = 4\frac{793}{1200}$
5. $4 \cdot -2\frac{1}{3} \cdot 2 = -18\frac{2}{3}$
6. $5\frac{1}{2} \div -3\frac{1}{6} = -1\frac{14}{19}$
7. $10 \div 2.5 \cdot -1\frac{2}{5} = -5\frac{3}{5}$
8. $3.6 \cdot -31.73 = -114.228$
9. $10.8 \div -2\frac{1}{2} \cdot 3\frac{1}{4} = -14\frac{1}{25}$
10. $2\frac{1}{7} \div -6.22 = -\frac{750}{2177}$
11. $-6.3 \cdot 2 \cdot \frac{1}{2} = -6.3$
12. $5\frac{1}{3} \cdot 9.80 \cdot 0 = 0$
13. $11 \cdot 4\frac{1}{12} \cdot -3 = -134\frac{3}{4}$
14. $(-3\frac{1}{4})(-3\frac{1}{4}) \div .4 = 26\frac{13}{32}$
15. $3\frac{1}{3} \div 1\frac{1}{2} \div \frac{5}{6} = 2\frac{2}{3}$
16. $10 \cdot 12.1 \cdot -6\frac{1}{6} = -746\frac{1}{6}$
17. $7.21 \cdot -2.37 = -17.0877$
18. $11.21 \cdot -7\frac{1}{3} \div 22\frac{5}{9} = -3\frac{6543}{10150}$

Name____________________ *Rational Numbers*

Multiplying and Dividing Rational Numbers

1. $1\frac{1}{14} \cdot -3\frac{2}{7} = -\frac{345}{98}$
2. $-6 \cdot 8\frac{2}{8} \cdot -1\frac{1}{4} = \frac{990}{16}$
3. $-5\frac{1}{6} \cdot 2\frac{7}{18} = -\frac{1333}{108}$
4. $3\frac{3}{8} \cdot 2.27 = 7.66125$
5. $2 \cdot -1\frac{1}{2} \cdot 5 = -15$
6. $3\frac{2}{3} \div -6\frac{1}{5} = -\frac{55}{93}$
7. $12 \div 2.2 \cdot -4\frac{4}{7} = -\frac{1920}{77}$
8. $4.2 \cdot -12.12 = -50.904$
9. $14.2 \div -6\frac{1}{5} \cdot 2\frac{2}{5} = -\frac{852}{155}$
10. $13.5 \div -3\frac{2}{3} \cdot 6\frac{3}{7} = -\frac{3645}{154}$
1. $12.8 \div -5\frac{2}{3} \cdot 2\frac{4}{5} = -6.324$
12. $5\frac{2}{5} \div -3.84 = -1\frac{13}{32}$
13. $-2.2 \cdot 5 \cdot \frac{1}{7} = -1\frac{4}{7}$
14. $6\frac{1}{5} \cdot 3.55 \cdot 0 = 0$
15. $13 \cdot 5\frac{1}{10} \cdot -2 = -132\frac{3}{5}$
16. $(-7\frac{2}{8})(-3\frac{2}{8}) \div .2 = 117\frac{13}{16}$
17. $2\frac{1}{5} \div 6\frac{3}{7} \div \frac{4}{6} = \frac{77}{150}$
18. $12 \cdot 13.3 \cdot -6\frac{1}{2} = -1037\frac{2}{5}$
19. $5.25 \cdot -3.89 = -20.4225$
20. $13.26 \cdot -8\frac{1}{3} \div 12\frac{5}{7} = -8\frac{123}{178}$
21. $10.10 \cdot -5\frac{1}{6} \div 20\frac{5}{6} = -2.504$ or $-2\frac{1895}{3750}$
22. $13.13 \cdot -13\frac{2}{6} \div 13\frac{1}{3} = -13.13$

Name____________________ *Rational Numbers*

Order of Operations with Rational Numbers

$-4 \cdot 3 + 2 = -12 + 2 = -14$

$2\frac{1}{3} \div (4 + 8) = \frac{7}{3} \div 12 = \frac{7}{3} \cdot \frac{1}{12} = \frac{7}{36}$

1. $-25 \div 6 + 4\frac{1}{5} = \frac{1}{30}$
2. $\frac{2}{3}(-15 - 4)$ $-12\frac{2}{3}$
3. $-8 \div -2 + 5 \cdot -\frac{1}{2} - 25 \div 5 = -\frac{7}{2}$
4. $\frac{1}{2}[(-15 + 4) + (6 + 7) \div -3] = -7\frac{2}{3}$
5. $(9\frac{1}{3} + 4\frac{1}{3}) \div 6 - -12 = 14\frac{5}{18}$
6. $\frac{(80 \div 4) + 25}{-12 + 35} = 1\frac{22}{23}$
7. $3[-3(2-10) - 5] = 57$
8. $2 \cdot 3[5 + (4 \div 2)] = 42$
9. $40 \div [(3 \cdot 3) - (36 \div 9)] + -81 = -73$

Answer Key

Name_______________________ *Rational Numbers*

Order of Operations with Rational Numbers

1. $-20 \div 3 + 2\frac{2}{3}$ = −4
2. $\frac{1}{4}(-12 + 6)$ = $-\frac{3}{2}$
3. $-5 \div -3 - 2 \cdot -\frac{1}{3} - 21 \div 7$ = $\frac{-2}{3}$
4. $\frac{1}{2}[(-12 - 2) + (1 + 8) \div -8]$ = $-7\frac{9}{16}$
5. $(5\frac{1}{5} - 2\frac{1}{5}) \cdot 6 - -16$ = 34
6. $\frac{(20 \div 2) + 10}{-10 + 20 + 30}$ = $\frac{1}{2}$
7. $2[-5(4 - 12) - 3]$ = 74
8. $4 \cdot 4[2 - (6 \div 3)]$ = 0
9. $20 \cdot [(3 \cdot 6) - (24 \div 8)] + -32$ = 268
10. $2 \div [(4 \div 2) + (32 \div 8)]$ = $\frac{1}{3}$
11. $[(2 \cdot 2) - (30 \div 6)] + -25 - 23$ = −49

Name_______________________ *Real Numbers*

Comparing Real Numbers

4.66 ____ 4.78		$4\frac{1}{2}$ ____ 4.78	
4.66 < 4.78		4.50 < 4.78	

Use <, >, or = to make each a true sentence.

1. 2.5 __=__ $2\frac{1}{2}$
2. 1.078 __<__ 1.78
3. 13.26 __<__ 132.6
4. 983.21 __<__ 7551.7
5. 232.33 __>__ 23.233
6. −.3 __<__ $-.\overline{3}$
7. $-9\frac{36}{48}$ __>__ −9.77
8. $12\frac{5}{8}$ __>__ 12.6
9. 1.5 __<__ $1\frac{2}{3}$
10. 3.2 __=__ $3\frac{1}{5}$

Rewrite any fractions as decimals, then put the decimals for each problem in order from least to greatest.

$2\frac{1}{2}$, $2\frac{3}{5}$, 2.4   2.4, $2\frac{1}{2}$, $2\frac{3}{5}$ 2.4, 2.5, 2.6

1. 2.51, 2.511, 2.5111   2.51, 2.511, 2.5111
2. $-3\frac{1}{5}$, $-3\frac{2}{3}$, $-3\frac{5}{7}$ −3.71, −3.66, −3.2
3. $-2\frac{1}{4}$, $2\frac{7}{8}$, $2\frac{3}{9}$ −2.25, 2.33, 2.88
4. $4\frac{2}{3}$, $-4\frac{6}{9}$, 4.34   −4.67, 4.34, 4.67
5. $-6\frac{1}{5}$, −6.66, $-6\frac{4}{5}$ −6.8, −6.66, −6.2
6. 10.78, 10.781, 10.710   10.710, 10.78, 10.781
7. $5\frac{1}{2}$, $5\frac{1}{3}$, $5\frac{3}{4}$ 5.33, 5.5, 5.75
8. $-1\frac{4}{5}$, $-1\frac{9}{10}$, $-1\frac{7}{8}$ −1.9, −1.88, −1.80
9. $7\frac{2}{3}$, 7.45, $7\frac{3}{5}$ 7.45, 7.6, 7.67
10. 3.15, 3.8, $3\frac{2}{5}$ 3.15, 3.4, 3.8

Name_______________________ *Equations*

Open Sentences

$\frac{1}{5} \cdot 10 = x$	$\frac{81}{9} - 12 = t$
$\frac{1}{\not{5}_1} \cdot \frac{\not{10}^2}{1} = x$	$9 - 12 = t$
$2 = x$	$-3 = t$

1. $\frac{15 + -7}{2} = r$ r = 4
2. $\frac{11 + 3}{7} = j$ j = 2
3. $\frac{2 + -18}{4} = p$ p = −4
4. $\frac{1}{5} \cdot -12 + -9 = w$ = $-11\frac{2}{5}$
5. $-7.5 \cdot 3.3 + 13 = g$ g = −11.75
6. $1\frac{3}{5} \div \frac{15}{45} = f$ f = $4\frac{4}{5}$
7. $4 \cdot 3.61 - 16.8 = n$ n = −2.36
8. $\frac{-25 + 12}{3} + 6 = b$ b = $\frac{5}{3}$
9. $-\frac{2}{5} \div \frac{1}{15} + -3\frac{1}{3} = y$ y = $-9\frac{1}{3}$
10. $\frac{6 - 12}{3} + 4 = p$ p = 2
11. $\frac{2}{6} \cdot 13 - 6 = m$ m = $-\frac{5}{3}$
12. $4.34 + 2.22 \div 3 = q$ q = 5.08
13. $-2 \cdot 5 - 6 = d$ d = −16
14. $1 + 2.78 - 6.5 = z$ z = −2.72

Name_______________________ *Equations*

Open Sentences

$26 = r \cdot 2$, if $r = 13$
$26 = 13 \cdot 2$
$26 = 26$ True

1. $6 + x = 3\frac{1}{3}$, if $x = -3\frac{1}{2}$ False
2. $2 + y = 9$, if $y = 6$ False
3. $\frac{m}{6} + -4 = 0$, if $m = 6$ False
4. $y(6 + 3) + 2 = 37$, if $y + 26$ False
5. $11.2 + .2 - r = 14.1$, if $r = 3.2$ False
6. $3x + 12 = 15$, if $x = -1$ False
7. $f(2 + 3) + 1 = 22$, if $f = 16$ False
8. $\frac{15 + 12}{b} + 6 = 15$, if $b = 3$ True
9. $-\frac{2}{5} \div \frac{1}{15} + c\frac{1}{3} = -3$, if $c = 2$ False
10. $7 + (e - 31) = -12$, if $e = -12$ False
11. $\frac{2}{6} \cdot 13 - k = 7$, if $k = 6$ False
12. $r + 6.32 \div 3 = 2.2$, if $r = -3$ False
13. $-t \cdot 5 - 6 = -23$, if $t = 5$ False
14. $z + 13 \div 6.5 = 7$, if $z = -3$ False

Answer Key

Name________________________ *Equations*

Evaluating Expressions

Evaluate the following if, $w = \frac{1}{2}$, $x = 3$, and $y = -4$

$2x(2w + 2y) = 2 \cdot 3\,[2(\tfrac{1}{2}) + 2(-4)] = 6(1 + -8) = 6(-7) = -42$

1. $w(xw + xy) = -\frac{21}{4}$
2. $3w - 4x = -\frac{21}{2}$
3. $5(w-2y) = \frac{85}{2}$
4. $y(w + 7) = -30$
5. $8x + -13x = -15$
6. $6(w + -y) = 27$
7. $5w(2y + 3x) = \frac{5}{2}$
8. $3w + 4(x - y) = 29\frac{1}{2}$
9. $w(xw + xy) = \frac{21}{4}$
10. $wx + x - 6xy = \frac{153}{2}$
11. $wx(3w + 2y - 5) = -\frac{69}{4}$
12. $6w - (xy + 3) = 12$
13. $4w - 7x + 3y - 2w = -32$
14. $12y(4y + 2w) + -2x = 714$

Name________________________ *Equations*

Simplifying Expressions

Distributive Property

$3(x + 4y) = 3x + 3 \cdot 4y = 3x + 12y$

1. $-6(b + c) = -6b + -6c$
2. $3(w - 4) = 3w - 12$
3. $2(x - 12) = 2x - 24$
4. $3(2 + r) = 6 + 3r$
5. $8(y + -2x) = 8y + -16x$
6. $5(n + 13y) = 5n + 65y$
7. $5(2y + 5x) = 10y + 25x$
8. $2(3p - 5p) = 6p - 10p$
9. $7(-c + 6d) = -7c + 42d$
10. $3(x + y + z) = 3x + 3y + 3z$
11. $4(2r + 6y) = 8r + 24y$
12. $3k(-xy + -5) = -3kxy + -15k$
13. $-9(2x + 8) = -18x - 72$
14. $12(2y + 5w) = 24y + 60w$

Name________________________ *Equations*

Simplifying Expressions

Distributive Property

$2(w + 2b) = 2w + 2 \cdot 2b = 2w + 4b$

1. $3(e + 3f) = 3e + 9f$
2. $6(2g + y) = 12g + 6y$
3. $7(y - 9) = 7y - 63$
4. $4(3 + k) = 12 + 4k$
5. $-5(h + -3p) = -5h + 15p$
6. $2(t - 6q) = 2t - 12q$
7. $-7(3s + 3m) = -21s + -21m$
8. $6(5d + 8b) = 30d + 48b$
9. $2(-t + 4e) = -2t + 8e$
10. $-4(j + k + g) = -4j + -4k + -4g$
11. $6(3v + 5c) = 18v + 30c$
12. $3d(-nm + 7) = -3dnm + 21d$
13. $-3(8g + 3a) = -24g + -9a$
14. $-5(3w + 8e) = -15w + -40e$

Name________________________ *Equations*

Simplifying Expressions

Combining like terms

$3n - 2n + 4r = (3 - 2)n + 4r$
$= n + 4r$

1. $7r + 2r - 4 = 9r - 4$
2. $23x - 7x + 4x = 20x$
3. $3xy + 13xy - 12xy = 4xy$
4. $-3n + 12 - 4n = -7n + 12$
5. $12ax - 2ax + 14x - 2a + -3x = 10ax + 11x - 2a$
6. $3x + 2y + xy - 6xy + 4x + -4y = 7x - 2y - 5xy$
7. $2r + 4ry - 5r + 3x - 4ry = -3r + 3x$
8. $12p + 5pd - 3p + 6pd = 9p + 11pd$
9. $4x - 2x + 6xy + 21x + -9xy - 9 = 23x + -3xy - 9$
10. $4e + 5ed + 4d - 7ed + 7 = 4e + 4d - 2ed + 7$
11. $3x + 2y - 2xy + 5x - 2xy = 8x - 4xy + 2y$
12. $7a + a - a + 3ab - ab + 2ab = 7a + 4ab$
13. $5m + 2m + 40m + m + 17 = 48m + 17$
14. $2x + 3xy + 4x + 5xy + 6x = 12x + 8xy$

Answer Key

Name________________________________ *Equations*

Simplifying Expressions

$5r - 3r + 4k = (5 - 3)r + 4k$
$= 2r + 4r$

1. $6r + 5r - 8p + 6p + 7(2r - 4r) =$ $-3r - 2p$
2. $9x - 7x + 2x + 8(6x + 2x) =$ $68x$
3. $5xy - 12xy + 12xy - 9(x + y) =$ $5xy - 9x - 9y$
4. $2t + 12t - 4(n + 4n) =$ $14t - 20n$
5. $-2(g + 5g) + -4(8f - -12g) =$ $-60g - 32f$
6. $7(2x + 5y) + xy - 6(3xy + 5x) =$ $-16x + 35y - 17xy$
7. $5m + 6mn - -9n + 2(m-n) =$ $7m + 6mn + 7n$
8. $12p + 5pd - 3p + 6pd =$ $9p + 11pd$
9. $3(x - 5x) + 2(xy + 8x) + -8xy =$ $4x - 6xy$
10. $-2a - -3(a + 7) - 4(-a + b) =$ $5a - 4b + 21$
11. $4n(x - y) + 3n(x + y) - 2 =$ $7nx - ny - 2$
12. $3(h - -k) + 2(-3h + -4k) =$ $-3h - 5k$
13. $8(2x + 2y) - 4(3xy - -5x) =$ $-4x + 16y - 12xy$
14. $3c - 4bc + -7b + 3(2bc - b) =$ $3c + 2bc - 10b$

Name________________________________ *Equations*

Solving Addition Equations

$1.6 = -3.6 + x$
$1.6 + 3.6 = -3.6 + 3.6 + x$
$5.2 = 0 + x$
$5.2 = x$

1. $x + -8 = 9$ — $x = 17$
2. $w + 79 = -95$ — $w = -174$
3. $5 + c = -16$ — $c = -21$
4. $-21 = t + 18$ — $t = -39$
5. $-14 + r = 23$ — $r = 37$
6. $3.5 = n + 4.6$ — $n = -1.1$
7. $-2\frac{1}{2} + k = -2\frac{5}{7}$ — $K = -\frac{3}{14}$
8. $-35 = x + 35$ — $x = -70$
9. $-\frac{1}{4} + x = -\frac{1}{4}$ — $x = 0$
10. $z + 4.2 = 9.1$ — $z = 4.9$
11. $28 = c + -14$ — $c = 42$
12. $x + -3\frac{3}{4} = -11\frac{1}{4}$ — $x = -7\frac{1}{2}$
13. $-2{,}929 + t = 4{,}383$ — $t = 7{,}312$
14. $-4.5 = 9\frac{1}{2} + c$ — $c = -14$

Name________________________________ *Equations*

Solving Subtraction Equations

$36 = x - -9$
$36 = x + 9$
$36 - 9 = x + 9 - 9$
$28 = x + 0$
$28 = x$

1. $x - 8 = 34$ — $x = 42$
2. $-33 = m - 11$ — $m = -22$
3. $t - -8 = 45$ — $t = 37$
4. $34 = b - -2$ — $b = 32$
5. $f - 16 = -32$ — $f = -16$
6. $-3.4 = h - 8.5$ — $h = 5.1$
7. $-3\frac{2}{3} - k = -6\frac{3}{4}$ — $K = 3\frac{1}{12}$
8. $-15 = p - 5$ — $p = -10$
9. $-\frac{1}{3} - g = -\frac{1}{3}$ — $g = 0$
10. $3.65 = n - 7$ — $n = 10.65$
11. $z - -23.5 = -2.342$ — $z = -25.842$
12. $a + -2\frac{1}{3} = -15\frac{1}{3}$ — $a = -13$
13. $-2{,}547 = n - 6{,}634$ — $n = 4{,}087$
14. $-2.2 = 8\frac{4}{5} - d$ — $d = 11$

Name________________________________ *Equations*

Solving Addition and Subtraction Equations

$12 = c - 9$
$12 = c - 9$
$12 + 9 = c - 9 + 9$
$21 = c + 0$
$21 = c$

1. $x + 4 = -22$ — $x = -26$
2. $51 = u - 12$ — $u = 63$
3. $b + -9 = 54$ — $b = 63$
4. $-56 = c - -8$ — $c = -64$
5. $t + 12 = -18$ — $t = -30$
6. $-6.7 = y - 27$ — $y = 20.3$
7. $-5\frac{3}{7} + t = -9\frac{4}{5}$ — $t = -4\frac{13}{35}$
8. $12.4 - k = 4.3$ — $k = 8.1$
9. $-\frac{3}{4} + j = -\frac{3}{7}$ — $j = \frac{9}{28}$
10. $5.77 = q + 9$ — $q = -3.23$
11. $w - -43.7 = -4.342$ — $w = -48.042$
12. $f + -3\frac{1}{4} = -12\frac{1}{4}$ — $f = -9$
13. $-3{,}282 = n + 1{,}111$ — $n = -4{,}393$
14. $-3.1 = 4\frac{3}{4} - e$ — $e = 7.85$

Answer Key

Name________________ *Equations*

Solving Multiplication Equations

$5y = -25$
$5 \div 5y = -25 \div 5$
$1y = -5$
$y = -5$

1. $-7b = -77$ — $b = 11$
2. $-144 = 12b$ — $b = -12$
3. $-15m = 15$ — $m = -1$
4. $36 = -6t$ — $t = -6$
5. $3.5 = 7x$ — $x = 0.5$
6. $-2.1 = -.7c$ — $c = 3$
7. $1\frac{2}{3} = 9x$ — $x = \frac{5}{27}$
8. $4m = -2$ — $m = -\frac{1}{2}$
9. $.24t = 1.2$ — $t = 5$
10. $-.0003 = .02c$ — $c = -0.015$
11. $-12n = -56$ — $n = 4\frac{2}{3}$
12. $43\frac{1}{2} = -13d$ — $d = -\frac{87}{26}$
13. $23.66 = 13r$ — $r = 1.82$
14. $33k = -878$ — $K = -\frac{878}{33}$

Name________________ *Equations*

Solving Multiplication Equations

$3y = -18$
$3 \div 3y = -18 \div 3$
$1y = -6$
$y = -6$

1. $9h = -81$ — $h = -9$
2. $60 = -5r$ — $r = -12$
3. $-11q = 11$ — $q = -1$
4. $42 = -7e$ — $e = -6$
5. $-4.5 = 9h$ — $h = -0.5$
6. $-6.7 = -.134k$ — $K = 50$
7. $2\frac{4}{6} = 5e$ — $e = \frac{8}{15}$
8. $15n = -3$ — $n = -\frac{1}{5}$
9. $.48y = 2.4$ — $y = 5$
10. $-.0009 = .03q$ — $q = -0.03$
11. $-13g = -65$ — $g = 5$
12. $28\frac{1}{3} = -12w$ — $w = -\frac{85}{36}$
13. $-350 = 25s$ — $s = -14$
14. $43u = -734$ — $u = -17\frac{3}{43}$

Name________________ *Equations*

Solving Division Equations

$\frac{x}{2} = 8$
$2 \cdot \frac{x}{2} = -8 \cdot 2$
$x = -16$

1. $-15 = \frac{x}{3}$ — $x = -45$
2. $\frac{u}{4} = -36$ — $u = -144$
3. $\frac{2}{3}c = -8$ — $c = -12$
4. $.9 = \frac{k}{81}$ — $K = 72.9$
5. $\frac{m}{6} = 36$ — $m = 216$
6. $\frac{1}{12}c = .6$ — $c = 7.2$
7. $\frac{1}{7}n = -28$ — $n = -196$
8. $-12 = \frac{t}{4}$ — $t = -48$
9. $\frac{x}{4.1} = 16$ — $x = 65.6$
10. $\frac{r}{17} = -23$ — $r = -391$
11. $-3 = \frac{1}{3}x$ — $x = -9$
12. $\frac{x}{8} = 56$ — $x = 448$
13. $\frac{3}{7}h = 4.5$ — $h = 10.5$
14. $\frac{2}{3}z = 33$ — $z = 49\frac{1}{2}$

Name________________ *Equations*

Solving Multiplication and Division Equations

$4y = -28$
$4 \div 4y = -28 \div 4$
$1y = -7$
$y = -7$

$\frac{n}{3} = 9$
$3 \cdot \frac{n}{3} = 9 \cdot 3$
$n = 27$

1. $5n = -75$ — $n = -15$
2. $12a = 144$ — $a = 12$
3. $-12r = 12$ — $r = -1$
4. $49 = -9u$ — $u = -5\frac{4}{9}$
5. $4.5 = 9y$ — $y = 0.5$
6. $3.7 = -.21w$ — $w = -17.619$
7. $2\frac{3}{5} = 6c$ — $c = \frac{13}{30}$
8. $-33 = \frac{t}{11}$ — $t = -363$
9. $\frac{f}{3.6} = 16$ — $f = 57.6$
10. $\frac{2}{12}b = -12$ — $b = -72$
11. $-6 = \frac{x}{6}$ — $x = -36$
12. $\frac{h}{9} = 63$ — $h = 567$
13. $\frac{2}{3}c = 5.9$ — $c = 8.85$
14. $\frac{1}{5}m = 22$ — $m = 110$

Answer Key

Name________________________ *Equations*

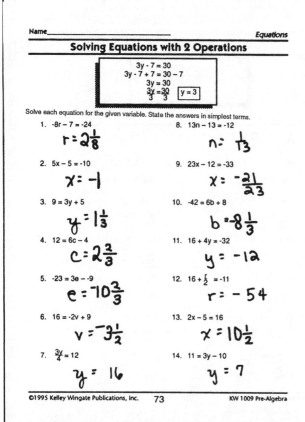

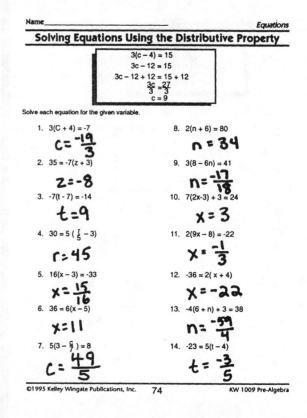

Solving Equations with 2 Operations

$3y - 7 = 30$
$3y - 7 + 7 = 30 - 7$
$3y = 30$
$\frac{3y}{3} = \frac{30}{3}$ $y = 3$

Solve each equation for the given variable. State the answers in simplest terms.

1. $-8r - 7 = -24$ — $r = 2\frac{1}{8}$
2. $5x - 5 = -10$ — $x = -1$
3. $9 = 3y + 5$ — $y = 1\frac{1}{3}$
4. $12 = 6c - 4$ — $c = 2\frac{2}{3}$
5. $-23 = 3e - -9$ — $e = -10\frac{2}{3}$
6. $16 = -2v + 9$ — $v = -3\frac{1}{2}$
7. $\frac{3y}{4} = 12$ — $y = 16$
8. $13n - 13 = -12$ — $n = \frac{1}{13}$
9. $23x - 12 = -33$ — $x = -\frac{21}{23}$
10. $-42 = 6b + 8$ — $b = -8\frac{1}{3}$
11. $16 + 4y = -32$ — $y = -12$
12. $16 + \frac{r}{2} = -11$ — $r = -54$
13. $2x - 5 = 16$ — $x = 10\frac{1}{2}$
14. $11 = 3y - 10$ — $y = 7$

Name________________________ *Equations*

Solving Equations Using the Distributive Property

$3(c - 4) = 15$
$3c - 12 = 15$
$3c - 12 + 12 = 15 + 12$
$\frac{3c}{3} = \frac{27}{3}$
$c = 9$

Solve each equation for the given variable.

1. $3(C + 4) = -7$ — $c = \frac{-19}{3}$
2. $35 = -7(z + 3)$ — $z = -8$
3. $-7(t - 7) = -14$ — $t = 9$
4. $30 = 5(\frac{r}{5} - 3)$ — $r = 45$
5. $16(x - 3) = -33$ — $x = \frac{15}{16}$
6. $36 = 6(x - 5)$ — $x = 11$
7. $5(3 - \frac{c}{7}) = 8$ — $c = \frac{49}{5}$
8. $2(n + 6) = 80$ — $n = 34$
9. $3(8 - 6n) = 41$ — $n = \frac{-17}{18}$
10. $7(2x - 3) + 3 = 24$ — $x = 3$
11. $2(9x - 8) = -22$ — $x = \frac{-1}{3}$
12. $-36 = 2(x + 4)$ — $x = -22$
13. $-4(6 + n) + 3 = 38$ — $n = \frac{-59}{4}$
14. $-23 = 5(t - 4)$ — $t = \frac{-3}{5}$

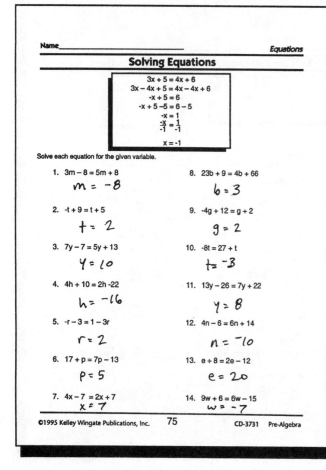

Name________________________ *Equations*

Solving Equations

$3x + 5 = 4x + 6$
$3x - 4x + 5 = 4x - 4x + 6$
$-x + 5 = 6$
$-x + 5 - 5 = 6 - 5$
$-x = 1$
$\frac{-x}{-1} = \frac{1}{-1}$
$x = -1$

Solve each equation for the given variable.

1. $3m - 8 = 5m + 8$ — $m = -8$
2. $-t + 9 = t + 5$ — $t = 2$
3. $7y - 7 = 5y + 13$ — $y = 10$
4. $4h + 10 = 2h - 22$ — $h = -16$
5. $-r - 3 = 1 - 3r$ — $r = 2$
6. $17 + p = 7p - 13$ — $p = 5$
7. $4x - 7 = 2x + 7$ — $x = 7$
8. $23b + 9 = 4b + 66$ — $b = 3$
9. $-4g + 12 = g + 2$ — $g = 2$
10. $-8t = 27 + t$ — $t = -3$
11. $13y - 26 = 7y + 22$ — $y = 8$
12. $4n - 6 = 6n + 14$ — $n = -10$
13. $e + 8 = 2e - 12$ — $e = 20$
14. $9w + 6 = 6w - 15$ — $w = -7$

Name________________________ *Equations*

Solving equation / Mixed Practice

Solve each equation for the given variable.

1. $-j + 5 = j - 7$ — $j = 6$
2. $9w + 9 = 3w - 15$ — $w = -4$
3. $3g + 12 = 6g - 3$ — $g = 5$
4. $45 = -9(e + 8)$ — $e = -13$
5. $4(y - 8) = -12$ — $y = 5$
6. $24 = 4(\frac{h}{2} - 7)$ — $h = 26$
7. $11g = 121$ — $g = 11$
8. $-13k = 52$ — $k = -4$
9. $35 = -7t$ — $t = -5$
10. $3h + 5 = 2h - 9$ — $h = -14$
11. $6u = 21 - u$ — $u = 3$
12. $12k + 13 = 8k + 33$ — $k = 5$
13. $7(9 - 6j) = -63$ — $j = 3$
14. $-6(36 - 10b) + 8 = 32$ — $b = 4$
15. $9(8c - 9) = -351$ — $c = 6$
16. $\frac{m}{2.5} = 22$ — $m = 55$
17. $\frac{2}{5}h = -20$ — $h = -50$
18. $-5 = \frac{b}{5}$ — $b = -25$

Answer Key

Name________________________ *Problem Solving*

Writing Algebraic Expressions

Three times a number decreased by 7	$3x - 7$
A number increased by 9	$x + 9$
The number divided by 3	$b \div 3$ or $\frac{b}{3}$
The product of 3 and 8	$3 \cdot 8$

1. Eleven times the sum of a number and five times the number $11(x+5x)$
2. Seven times the sum of twice a number and sixteen $7(2x+16)$
3. Eleven times a number decreased by three $11x-3$
4. Two-fifths of a number minus seven $\frac{2}{5}x-7$
5. Three times the difference between x and 5 $3(x-5)$
6. Five times a number plus six times the number $5x+6x$
7. A number increased by three times the number $x+3x$
8. The quotient of a number and five decreased by two $\frac{x}{5}-2$
9. One-third times a number increased by six $\frac{1}{3}x+6$
10. Four times the sum of a number and eight $4(x+8)$
11. Five increased by seven times a number $5+7x$
12. The product of six and a number increased by six $6(x+6)$

Name________________________ *Problem Solving*

Writing Algebraic Expressions

Three times a number decreased by 7	$3x - 7$
A number increased by 9	$x + 9$
The number divided by 3	$b \div 3$ or $\frac{b}{3}$
The product of 3 and 8	$3 \cdot 8$

1. Two-thirds of a number and eight $\frac{2}{3}x+8$
2. Nine more than the quotient of b and 4 $(b \div 4)+9$
3. Two times the sum of a number and twelve $2(x+12)$
4. Four-sevenths of a number minus six $\frac{4}{7}x-6$
5. three times a number plus five times the number $3x+5x$
6. Seven times the difference between c and 4 $7(c-4)$
7. A number increased by four times the number $x+4x$
8. The quotient of a number and four increased by three $(x \div 4)+3$
9. two-thirds times a number increased by five $\frac{2}{3}x+5$
10. Two times a number times and eight $2x+8$
11. Three increased by two times a number $3+2x$
12. The quotient of five and a number increased by two $(5 \div x)+2$

Name________________________ *Problem Solving*

Writing Algebraic Expressions

Write an equation for each and solve.

> Nine more than a number is 35. Find the number.
>
> $9 + x = 35$
>
> $9 - 9 + x = 35 - 9$
>
> $x = 26$

1. A number increased by 7 is -23. Find the number. $x+7=-23$; $x=-30$
2. One-third of a number is -20. Find the number. $\frac{1}{3}x=-20$; $x=-60$
3. The product of -7 and a number is 35. Find the number. $-7x=35$; $x=-5$
4. Three times a number is 21. Find the number. $3x=21$; $x=7$
5. The cost of five cakes is \$41.00. What is the cost of each cake? $5x=41$; $x=\$8.20$
6. The cost of a saddle is \$231.00. What is the cost of four saddles? $(231)(4)=x$; $\$924=x$
7. Four times a number is 52. Find the number. $4x=52$; $x=13$

Name________________________ *Problem Solving*

Writing Algebraic Expressions

Write an equation for each and solve.

> Eight more than a number is 28. Find the number.
>
> $8 + x = 28$
>
> $8 - 8 + x = 28 - 8$
>
> $x = 20$

1. A number increased by 9 is 41. Find the number. $x+9=41$; $x=32$
2. One-fourth of a number is 12. Find the number. $\frac{1}{4}x=12$; $x=48$
3. The product of -4 and a number is 36. Find the number. $-4x=36$; $x=-9$
4. Three times a number is 45. Find the number. $3x=45$; $x=15$
5. The cost of five boxes is \$22.00. What is the cost of each box? $5x=22$; $x=\$4.40$
6. The cost of a television is \$432.00. What is the cost of four televisions? $(4)(432)=x$; $\$1728=x$
7. Four times a number is 48. Find the number. $4x=48$; $x=12$

Answer Key

Name________________________ *Problem Solving*

Writing Algebraic Expressions

Write an equation for each and solve.

> Six more than 3 times a number is 21.
> What is the number?
>
> $6 + 3x = 21$
> $6 - 6 + 3x = 21 - 6$
> $3x = 15$
> $x = 5$

1. Two-thirds of a number increased by two is ten. What is the number?

   $\frac{2}{3}x+2=10 \quad x=12$

2. Six more than a number is negative thirty-one. What is the number?

   $6+x=-31 \quad x=-37$

3. Nine less than three times a number is twenty-seven. What is the number?

   $3x-9=27 \quad x=12$

4. Two times the sum of a number and five is twenty-six. What is the number?

   $2(x+5)=26 \quad x=8$

5. The product of a number and four increased by seven is three. What is the number?

   $4x+7=3 \quad x=-1$

6. The quotient of a number and three decreased by six is two. What is the number?

   $\frac{x}{3}-6=2 \quad x=24$

7. Two more than five times a number is thirty-two. What is the number?

   $2+5x=32 \quad x=6$

Name________________________ *Problem Solving*

Writing Algebraic Expressions

Write an equation for each and solve for the variable.

> One number plus 5 times that number equals 120.
> Find the number.
>
> $x + 5x = 120$
> $6x = 120$
> $x = 20$

1. One number plus six times that number equals 133. Find the number.

   $x+6x=133$ (19)

2. The sum of two numbers is 36. The larger number is twice the smaller number. Find the number.

   $x+2x=36$ (12)

3. One number plus three times that number is 44. Find the number.

   $x+3x=44$ (11)

4. The difference between two numbers is 16. The first number is five times the second number. Find the number.

   $5x-x=16$ (4)

5. One number is seven times a second number. Four times the smaller number plus twice the larger number equals 36. Find the number.

   $4(x)+2(7x)=36$ (2)

6. There were 474 tickets sold for the school football game. Students bought five times as many tickets as the faculty did. Find the number of student and faculty tickets sold.

   $5f+f=474$ Students-395 / faculty 79

7. The sum of two numbers is 126. The larger number is 5 times larger than the smaller number. Find the number.

   $x+5x=126$ (21)

Name________________________ *Problem Solving*

Writing Algebraic Expressions

Write an equation for each and solve.

> Seven times a number equals fifteen less than two times the number. Find the number.
>
> $7x = 2x - 15$
> $7x - 2x = 2x - 2x - 15$
> $5x = -15$
> $x = -3$

1. One half of a number is 12 more than 2 times the number. Find the number.

   $\frac{1}{2}x=12+2x \quad x=-8$

2. Thirty decreased by three times a number is six less than three times the number. Find the number.

   $30-3x=3x-6 \quad x=6$

3. Fifty increased by five times a number is six less than four times the number. Find the number.

   $50+5x=4x-6 \quad x=^{-}56$

4. Twice a number decreased by 39 is five times the sum of the number and two times the number. Find the number.

   $2x-39=5(x+2x) \quad x=-3$

5. Twelve increased by six times a number is six less than seven times the number. Find the number.

   $12+6x=7x-6 \quad x=18$

6. Nineteen increased by three times a number is four less than four times the number. Find the number.

   $19+3x=4x-4 \quad x=23$

7. Four times the sum of a number and three is seven times the number decreased by 3. Find the number.

   $4(x+3)=7x-3 = x=5$

Name________________________ *Inequalities*

Number Lines

$s \geq 4$

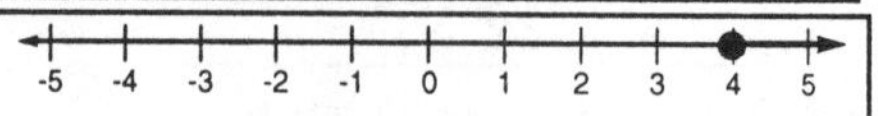

$b \geq 2$

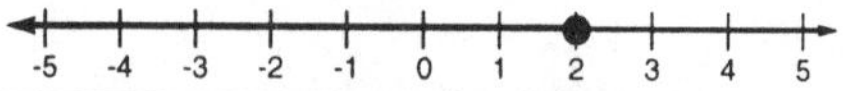

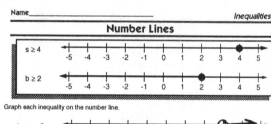

Graph each inequality on the number line.

1. $a > 3$

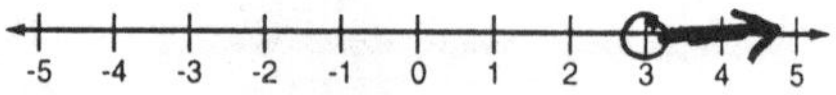

2. $b > -2$

3. $w \geq 3$

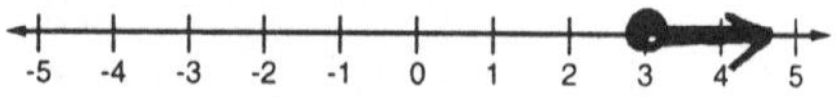

4. $k \leq -2$

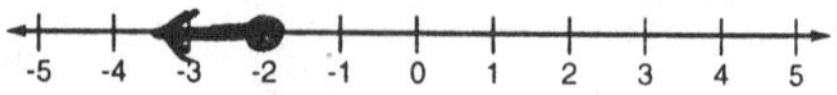

5. $n \geq -2$

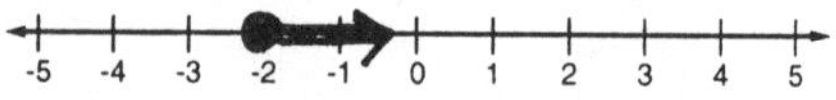

6. $y \leq 4$

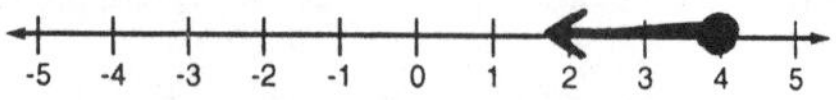

7. $r > \frac{2}{3}$

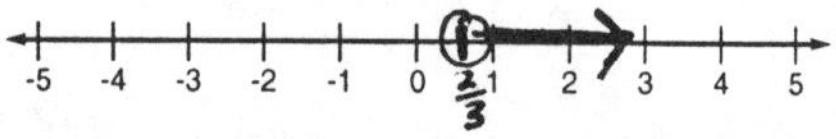

8. $x \geq -\frac{1}{2}$

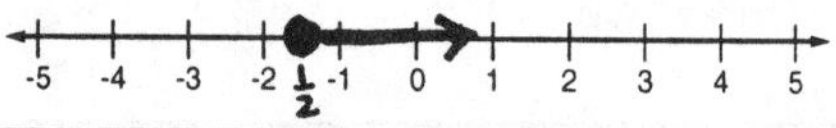

Answer Key

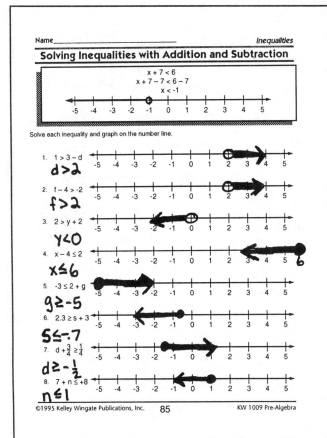

Name______________________ *Inequalities*

Solving Inequalities with Addition and Subtraction

x + 7 < 6
x + 7 − 7 < 6 − 7
x < -1

Solve each inequality and graph on the number line.

1. 1 > 3 − d
d>2
2. f − 4 > -2
f>2
3. 2 > y + 2
y<0
4. x − 4 ≤ 2
x≤6
5. -3 ≤ 2 + g
g≥-5
6. 2.3 ≥ s + 3
s≤-.7
7. d + $\frac{3}{4}$ ≥ $\frac{1}{4}$
d≥-$\frac{1}{2}$
8. 7 + n ≤ +8
n≤1

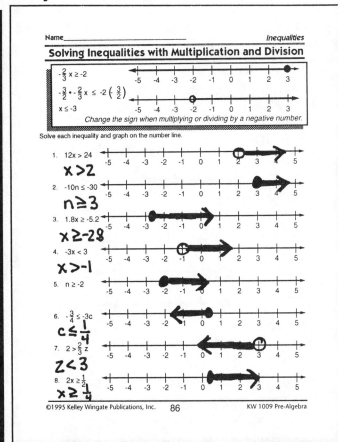

Name______________________ *Inequalities*

Solving Inequalities with Multiplication and Division

-$\frac{2}{3}$x ≥ -2

-$\frac{3}{2}$ • -$\frac{2}{3}$x ≤ -2(-$\frac{3}{2}$)

x ≤ -3

Change the sign when multiplying or dividing by a negative number.

Solve each inequality and graph on the number line.

1. 12x > 24
x>2
2. -10n ≤ -30
n≥3
3. 1.8x ≥ -5.2
x≥-2.8
4. -3x < 3
x>-1
5. n ≥ -2
6. -$\frac{3}{4}$ ≤ -3c
c≤$\frac{1}{4}$
7. 2 > $\frac{2}{3}$z
z<3
8. 2x ≥ $\frac{1}{2}$
x≥$\frac{1}{4}$

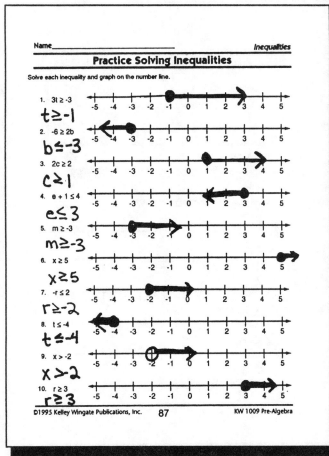

Name______________________ *Inequalities*

Practice Solving Inequalities

Solve each inequality and graph on the number line.

1. 3t ≥ -3
t≥-1
2. -6 ≥ 2b
b≤-3
3. 2c ≥ 2
c≥1
4. e + 1 ≤ 4
e≤3
5. m ≥ -3
m≥-3
6. x ≥ 5
x≥5
7. -r ≤ 2
r≥-2
8. t ≤ -4
t≤-4
9. x > -2
x>-2
10. r ≥ 3
r≥3

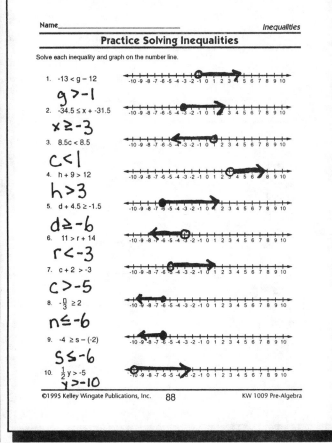

Name______________________ *Inequalities*

Practice Solving Inequalities

Solve each inequality and graph on the number line.

1. -13 < g − 12
g>-1
2. -34.5 ≤ x + -31.5
x≥-3
3. 8.5c < 8.5
c<1
4. h + 9 > 12
h>3
5. d + 4.5 ≥ -1.5
d≥-6
6. 11 > r + 14
r<-3
7. c + 2 > -3
c>-5
8. -$\frac{n}{3}$ ≥ 2
n≤-6
9. -4 ≥ s − (-2)
s≤-6
10. $\frac{1}{2}$y > -5
y>-10

Answer Key

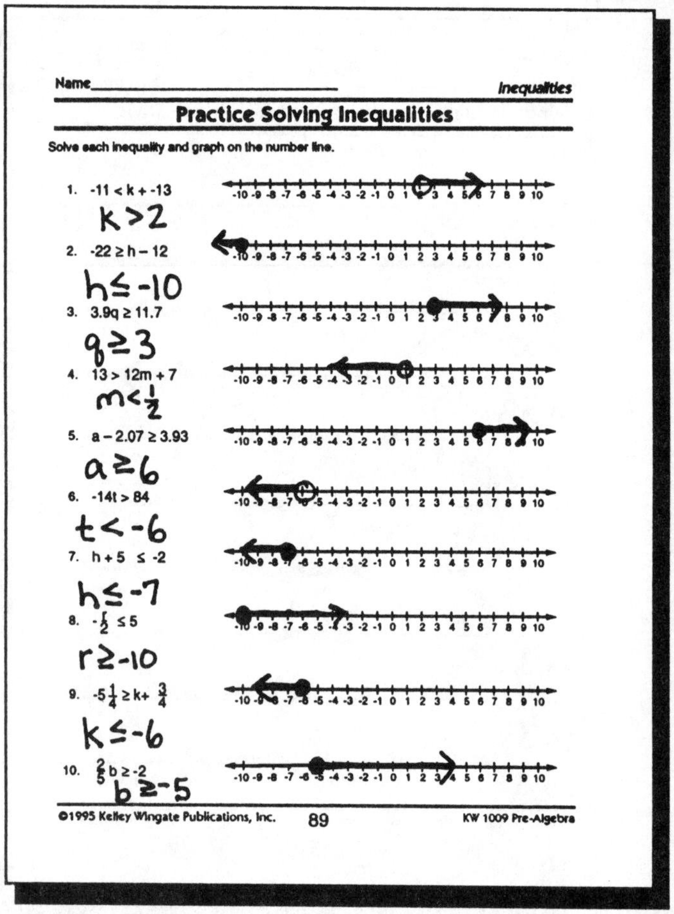

Name________________ *Inequalities*

Practice Solving Inequalities

Solve each inequality and graph on the number line.

1. $-11 < k + -13$ — $k > 2$
2. $-22 \geq h - 12$ — $h \leq -10$
3. $3.9q \geq 11.7$ — $q \geq 3$
4. $13 > 12m + 7$ — $m < \frac{1}{2}$
5. $a - 2.07 \geq 3.93$ — $a \geq 6$
6. $-14t > 84$ — $t < -6$
7. $h + 5 \leq -2$ — $h \leq -7$
8. $-\frac{r}{2} \leq 5$ — $r \geq -10$
9. $-5\frac{1}{4} \geq k + \frac{3}{4}$ — $k \leq -6$
10. $\frac{2}{5}b \geq -2$ — $b \geq -5$

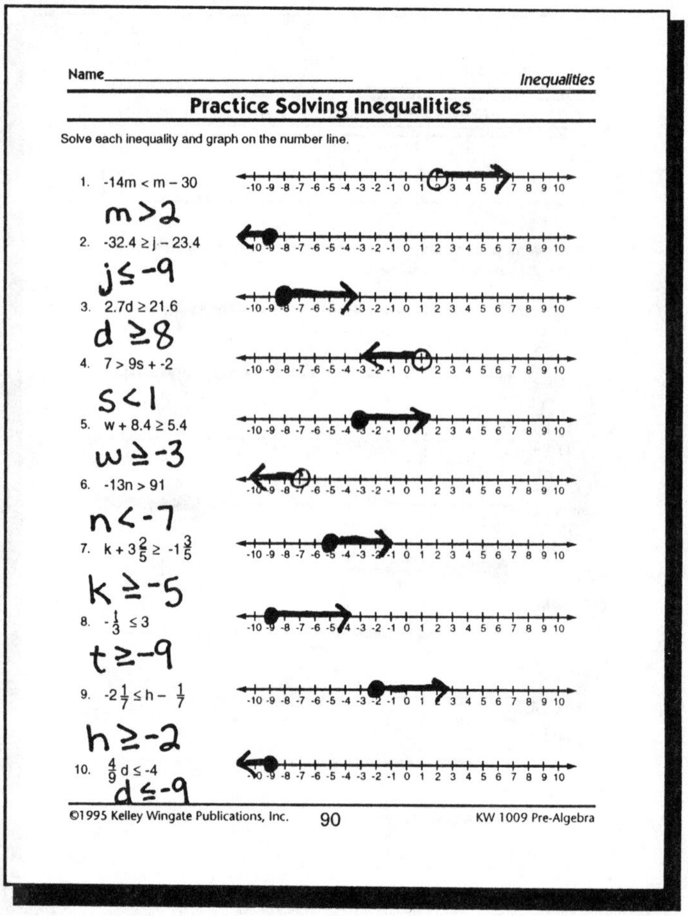

Name________________ *Inequalities*

Practice Solving Inequalities

Solve each inequality and graph on the number line.

1. $-14m < m - 30$ — $m > 2$
2. $-32.4 \geq j - 23.4$ — $j \leq -9$
3. $2.7d \geq 21.6$ — $d \geq 8$
4. $7 > 9s + -2$ — $s < 1$
5. $w + 8.4 \geq 5.4$ — $w \geq -3$
6. $-13n > 91$ — $n < -7$
7. $k + 3\frac{2}{5} \geq -1\frac{3}{5}$ — $k \geq -5$
8. $-\frac{t}{3} \leq 3$ — $t \geq -9$
9. $-2\frac{1}{7} \leq h - \frac{1}{7}$ — $h \geq -2$
10. $\frac{4}{9}d \leq -4$ — $d \leq -9$

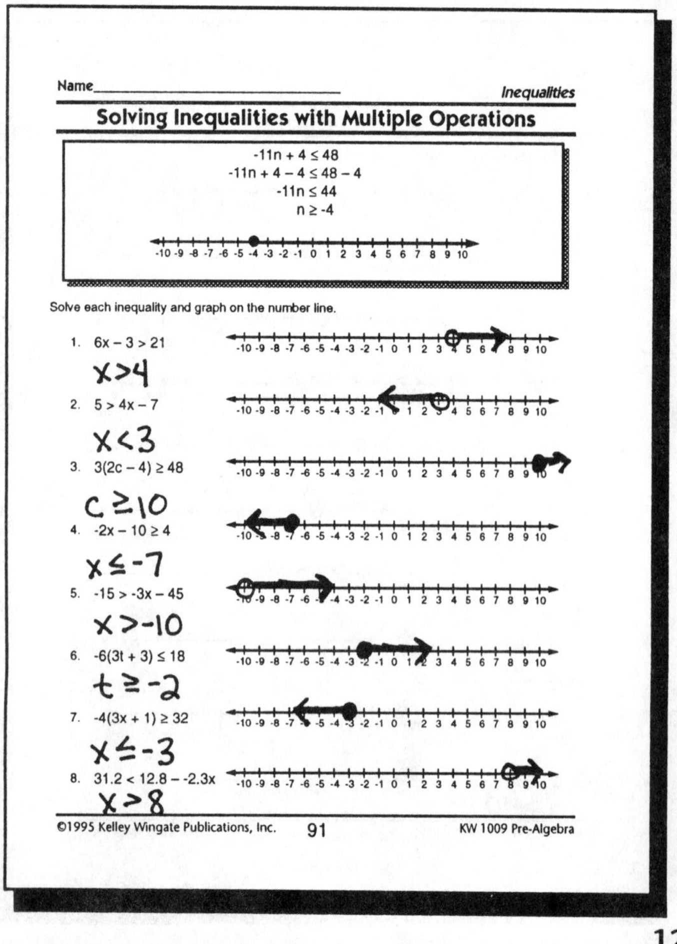

Name________________ *Inequalities*

Solving Inequalities with Multiple Operations

$-11n + 4 \leq 48$
$-11n + 4 - 4 \leq 48 - 4$
$-11n \leq 44$
$n \geq -4$

Solve each inequality and graph on the number line.

1. $6x - 3 > 21$ — $x > 4$
2. $5 > 4x - 7$ — $x < 3$
3. $3(2c - 4) \geq 48$ — $c \geq 10$
4. $-2x - 10 \geq 4$ — $x \leq -7$
5. $-15 > -3x - 45$ — $x > -10$
6. $-6(3t + 3) \leq 18$ — $t \geq -2$
7. $-4(3x + 1) \geq 32$ — $x \leq -3$
8. $31.2 < 12.8 - -2.3x$ — $x > 8$

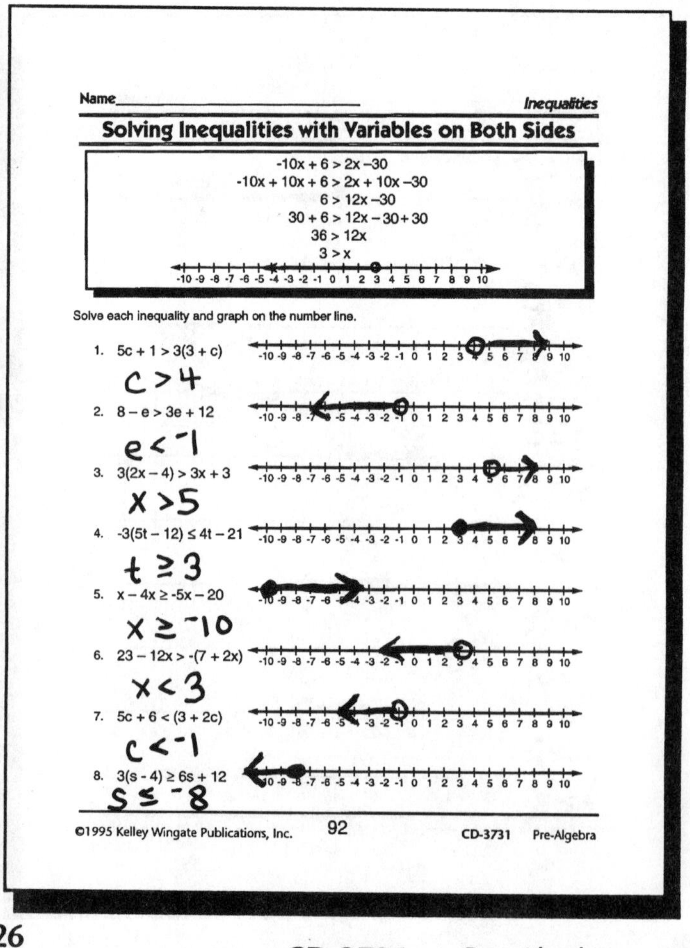

Name________________ *Inequalities*

Solving Inequalities with Variables on Both Sides

$-10x + 6 > 2x - 30$
$-10x + 10x + 6 > 2x + 10x - 30$
$6 > 12x - 30$
$30 + 6 > 12x - 30 + 30$
$36 > 12x$
$3 > x$

Solve each inequality and graph on the number line.

1. $5c + 1 > 3(3 + c)$ — $c > 4$
2. $8 - e > 3e + 12$ — $e < {}^{-}1$
3. $3(2x - 4) > 3x + 3$ — $x > 5$
4. $-3(5t - 12) \leq 4t - 21$ — $t \geq 3$
5. $x - 4x \geq -5x - 20$ — $x \geq {}^{-}10$
6. $23 - 12x > -(7 + 2x)$ — $x < 3$
7. $5c + 6 < (3 + 2c)$ — $c < {}^{-}1$
8. $3(s - 4) \geq 6s + 12$ — $s \leq {}^{-}8$

Answer Key

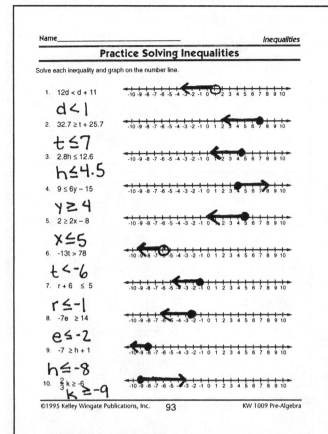

Name________________________ *Inequalities*

Practice Solving Inequalities

Solve each inequality and graph on the number line.

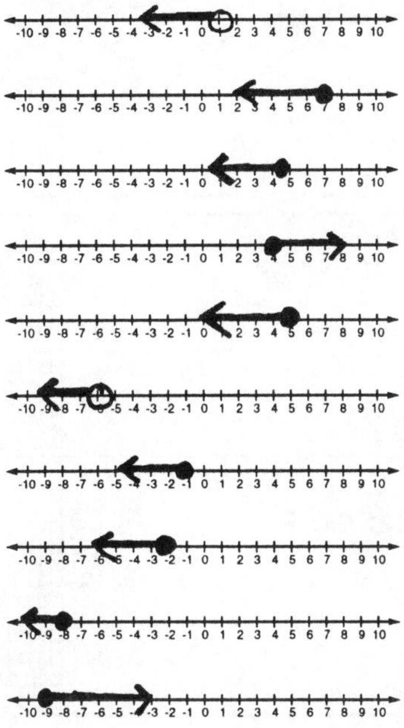

1. 12d < d + 11
   d<1
2. 32.7 ≥ t + 25.7
   t≤7
3. 2.8h ≤ 12.6
   h≤4.5
4. 9 ≤ 6y – 15
   y≥4
5. 2 ≥ 2x – 8
   x≤5
6. -13t > 78
   t<-6
7. r + 6 ≤ 5
   r≤-1
8. -7e ≥ 14
   e≤-2
9. -7 ≥ h + 1
   h≤-8
10. $\frac{2}{3}$k ≥ -6
   k≥-9

Name________________________ *Inequalities*

Practice Solving Inequalities

Solve each inequality and graph on the number line.

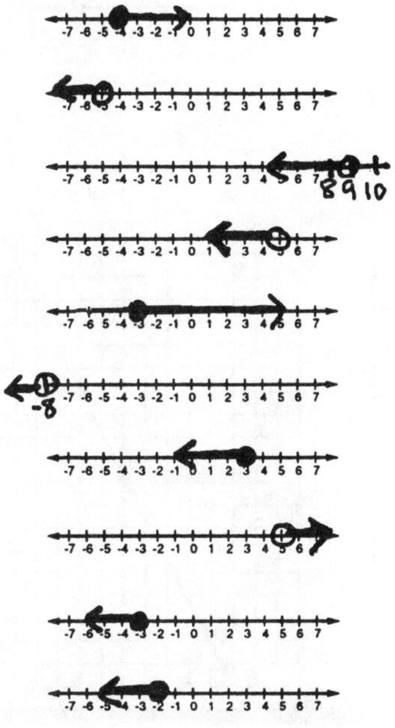

1. 2(3a + 4) ≥ 3a – 4
   a≥-4
2. 4x + 7 < x – 8
   x<-5
3. 5(3w – 4) < 12w + 7
   w<9
4. 8c – 7 + c < 13 + 5c
   c<5
5. 13x ≥ -39
   x≥-3
6. 48 > x + 56
   x<-8
7. 12 (m–1) ≤ 5(m + 3) –6
   m≤3
8. $\frac{1}{2} < \frac{1}{2}$x – 2
   x>5
9. -5(4a + 4) ≥ 40
   a≤-3
10. 3(4c + 3) + 1 ≤ 2 (c–5)
   c≤-2

Name________________________ *Ordered Pairs and Graphing*

Plotting Points

(x,y) = (1, -2) Over 1 and down 2
(x,y) = (-3, 4) Over 3 and up 4
(x,y) = (2, -2) Over 2 and down 2

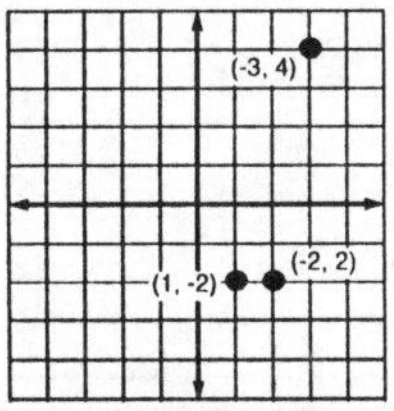

Identify the following points.

A (2, -6)
B (1, -3)
C (-3, -3)
D (6, -4)
E (0, -5)
F (5, 0)
G (6, 5)
H (7, 1)
I (4, 3)
J (2, 3)

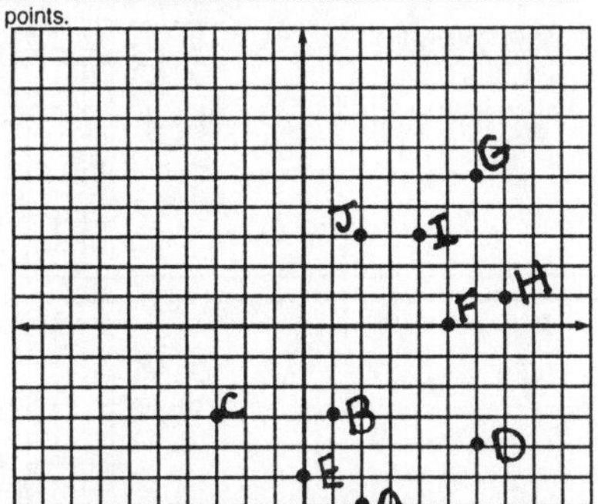

Name________________________ *Ordered Pairs and Graphing*

Plotting Points

y – 3 = 4x
y – 3 + 3 = 4x + 3
y = 4x + 3

Let x = -2, 1, 2
Solve for y

x = -2	x = 1	x = 2
y = 4 • -2 + 3	y = 4 • 1 + 3	y = 4 • 2 + 3
y = -8 + 3	y = 7 + 3	y = 8 + 3
y = -5	y = 10	y = 11
(-2, -5)	(1, 10)	(2, 11)

Solve each equation for y. Use the given values for x to find the values for y. Write answers as ordered pairs.

1. 6x + y = 3 y = -6x + 3 Let x = -4, 0, 2 (-4,27) (0,3) (2,-9)
2. -x = y – 4 y = -x + 4 Let x = -1, -2, -3 (-1,5),(-2,6) (-3,7)
3. 4 – y = 3x y = -3x + 4 Let x = -3, 1, -2 (-3,13) (1, 1) (-2,10)
4. 6x – y = -12 y = 6x + 12 Let x = 2, 3, -2 (2,24),(3,30)(-2,0)
5. 2x + y = -8 y = -2x - 8 Let x = -3, 2, 4 (-3,-2) (2,-12) (4,-16)
6. 2 = y – 4x y = 4x + 2 Let x = -1, 0, 2 (-1,-2) (0,2) (2,10)
7. 2x + y = -14 y = -2x + -14 Let x = -2, 0, 3 (-2,-10) (0,-14) (3,-20)

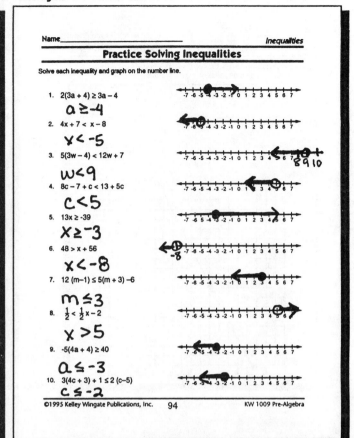

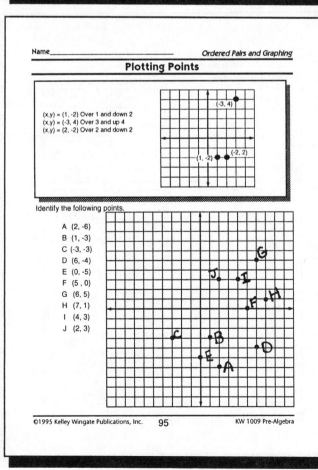

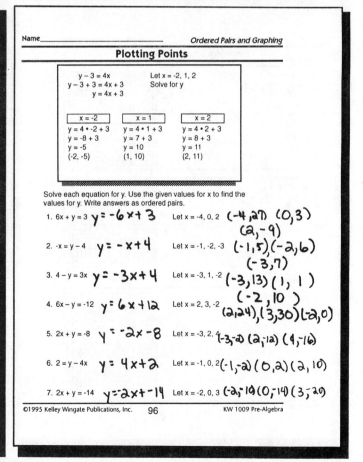

Answer Key

Name______________________________ *Ordered Pairs and Graphing*

Graphing Linear Equations

Solve for y in each equation. Choose 3 values for x and find the values for y. Graph the 3 ordered pairs and draw a line connecting them.

y – 5 = 2x
y – 5 + 5 = 2x + 5
y = 2x + 3

x	y
-2	-1
0	3
1	9

y = 2 • -2 + 3
y = -4 + 3
y = -1

y = 2 • 0 + 3
y = 0 + 3
y = 3

y = 2 • 1 + 3
y = 2 + 3
y = 5

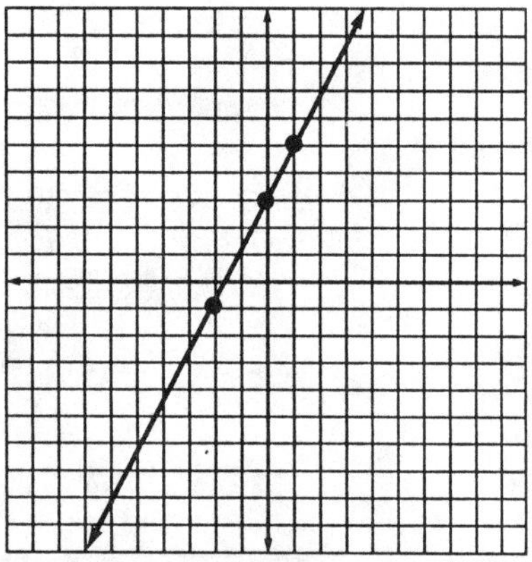

Name______________________________ *Ordered Pairs and Graphing*

Graphing Linear Equations

1. y – 4 = 2x

y = 2x+4

x	y
-1	2
-2	0
0	4

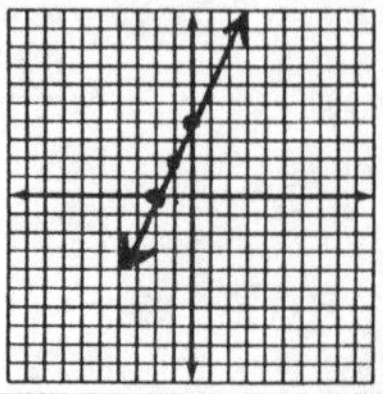

2. 3x + y = -5

y = -3x – 5

x	y
0	-5
-1	-2
-2	1

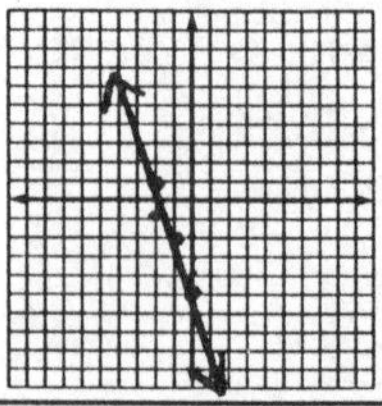

3. y + 8 = 5x

y = 5x – 8

x	y
0	-8
1	-3
2	2

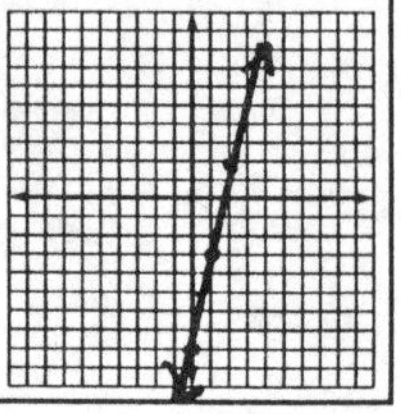

Name______________________________ *Ordered Pairs and Graphing*

Graphing Linear Equations

1. 3x – y = 3

y = 3x – 3

x	y
0	-3
1	0
-1	-6

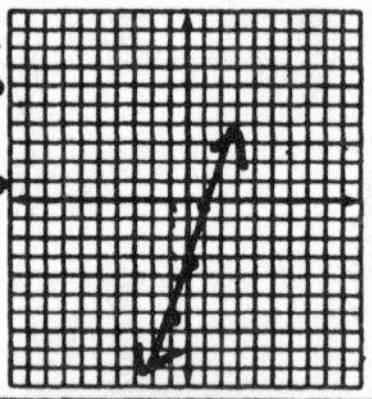

2. 5x – y = 7

y = 5x – 7

x	y
0	-7
1	-2
2	3

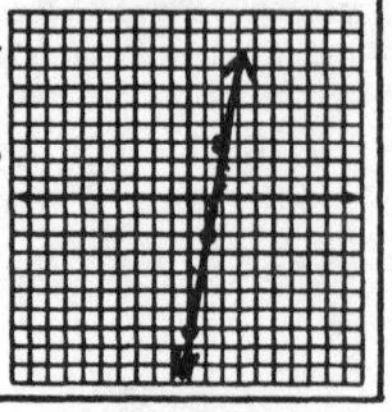

3. y = -3x – 5

x	y
0	-5
-1	-2
-2	1

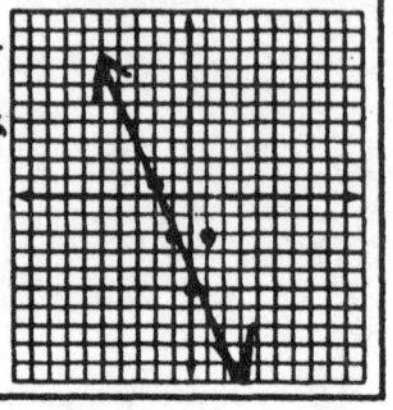

Name______________________________ *Ordered Pairs and Graphing*

Graphing Linear Equations

1. $\frac{3}{4}x + y = 2$

$y = -\frac{3}{4}x + 2$

x	y
0	2
4	-1
8	-4

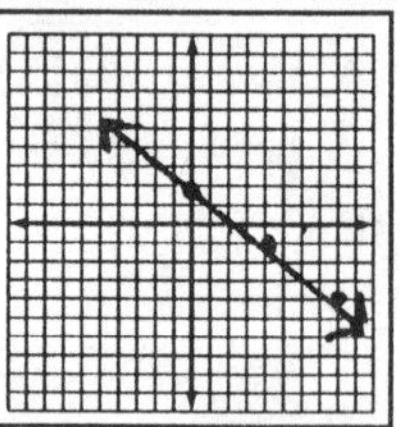

2. x – y = -2

y = x + 2

x	y
0	2
-2	0
-1	1

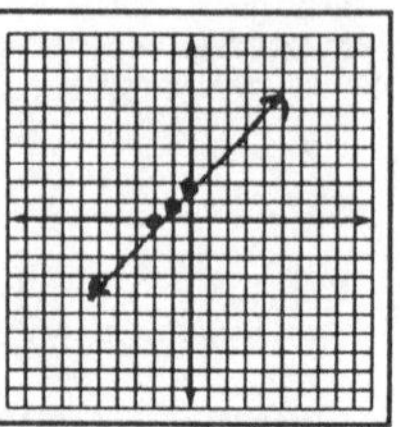

3. -2x + y = -5

y = 2x – 5

x	y
0	-5
1	-3
2	-1

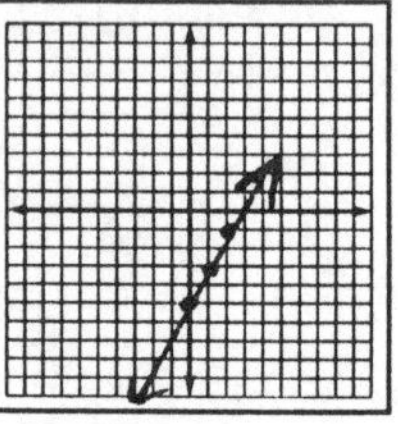

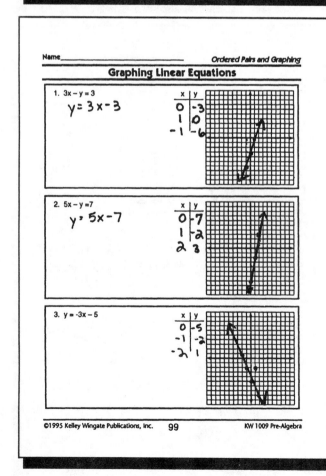

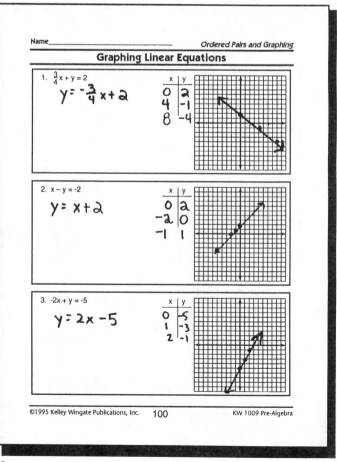

Keep up the Great Work!

______________________ **earns this award for**

____

You are TERRIFIC!

______________________________ ____________

Signed Date

Certificate of Completion

This certificate certifies that

____

Has completed

____

______________________________ Signed

__________ Date

Write as a fraction: 0.27	Write as a fraction: 0.008	Write as a fraction: 0.55	Write as a fraction: 0.95
Write as a fraction: 0.01	Write as a fraction: 0.4	Write as a fraction: 0.025	Write as a fraction: 0.9
Write as a decimal: $\frac{3}{4}$	Write as a decimal: $\frac{1}{8}$	Write as a decimal: $\frac{2}{3}$	Write as a decimal: $\frac{4}{5}$
Write as a decimal: $\frac{3}{10}$	Write as a decimal: $\frac{11}{100}$	Write as a decimal: $\frac{13}{20}$	Write as a decimal: $\frac{9}{1000}$

$\frac{19}{20}$	$\frac{11}{20}$	$\frac{1}{125}$	$\frac{27}{100}$
$\frac{9}{10}$	$\frac{1}{40}$	$\frac{2}{5}$	$\frac{1}{100}$
0.8	0.6	0.125	0.75
0.009	0.65	0.11	.3

Round to the nearest tenth: **85.62**	Round to the nearest tenth: **403.13**	Round to the nearest tenth: **1,749.27**	Round to the nearest tenth: **3.86**
Round to the nearest hundredth: **5.376**	Round to the nearest hundredth: **2,498.943**	Round to the nearest hundredth: **167.890**	Round to the nearest hundredth: **13.807**
Round to the nearest whole number: **82.61**	Round to the nearest whole number: **749.3**	Round to the nearest whole number: **3,914.521**	Round to the nearest whole number: **407.09**
Round to the nearest ten: **837.3**	Round to the nearest ten: **4,492**	Round to the nearest hundred: **421,948**	Round to the nearest hundred: **37,353.4**

3.9	1,749.3	403.1	85.6
13.81	167.89	2,498.94	5.38
407	3.915	749	83
37,400	421,900	4,490	840

$(-8)(-4) =$	$-7 \times (-3) =$	$42 \div (-7) =$	$-54 \div 9 =$
$(-5) \bullet (7) =$	$-72 \div (-8) =$	$-36 \div -12 =$	$3 \times (-4) =$
$63 \div (-7) =$	$(5)(-5) =$	$48 \div (-6) =$	$-20 \div 4 =$
$-12 \bullet 8 =$	$(-11)(12) =$	$(-24) \div (-12) =$	$(4)(-12) =$

-6	-6	21	32
-12	3	9	-35
-5	-8	-25	-9
-48	2	-132	-96

$-6 - 4 =$	$3 - 12 =$	$-7 - (-7) =$	$4 + 9 =$
$-14 - (-6) =$	$8 - 16 =$	$9 - (-6) =$	$-15 - (-8) =$
$-9 + 6 =$	$-4 - 4 =$	$-8 + (-6) =$	$2 - 8 =$
$4 - (-3) =$	$9 - 15 =$	$-6 - (-10) =$	$-3 - (-6) =$

13	0	-9	-10
-7	15	-8	-8
-6	-14	-8	-3
3	4	-6	7

$7 + 2 \times 3 =$	$15 \div 3 \times 8 =$	$12 - 4 + 6 =$	$2(8 + 3)$
$25 \div 5 - 3 =$	$9 + 8 \div 4$	$3 \bullet 4 - 2 \bullet 6 =$	$7 - 42 \div 7 =$
$5 + 3(14 \div 2)$	$45 \div 5 + 7 =$	$8 + 4 \bullet 2 =$	$24 \div (3 + 5) =$
$4^2 - 3 \bullet 5$	$(7 + 2)^2 =$	$16 \div 4 \times 3 =$	$72 \div 2^3 - 3 =$

22	14	40	13
1	0	11	2
3	16	16	26
6	12	81	1